Napoleon Bonaparte's First Campaign

Napoleon Bonaparte's First Campaign

Italy 1796-97 and the defeat
of the Austrian armies

Herbert H. Sargent

LEONAUR

Napoleon Bonaparte's
First Campaign
Italy 1796-97 and the defeat
of the Austrian armies
by Herbert H. Sargent

First published under the title
Napoleon Bonaparte's First Campaign

Leonaur is an imprint
of Oakpast Ltd

ISBN: 978-0-85706-190-4(hardcover)
ISBN: 978-0-85706-189-8 (softcover)

http://www.leonaur.com

Publisher's Notes

Contents

To
Victor M. Gore
This Book is Dedicated by the Author
In Remembrance of the Days of
Our Boyhood Together
In Illinois.

Preface

The matter contained in this book has been obtained by a study of military histories and the art and science of war as set forth in the writings of others. My thanks are due to Professor A. S. Hill, of Harvard College, to Professor George L. Andrews, Colonel (retired) U. S. Army, and especially to Jos. B. Batchelor, Jr., First Lieutenant Twenty-fourth Infantry, U. S. Army, for suggestions and criticisms in the composition of this book.

H. H. S.

Fort Bowie, Arizona,
September 29, 1894.

There is no genius like the genius of labour. There is no reward like that which comes from energy, system, and perseverance.

Introduction

Nothing is attained in war except by calculation. During a campaign, whatever is not profoundly considered in all its details is without result. Every enterprise should be conducted according to a system; chance alone can never bring success.—Napoleon.

To obtain a knowledge of the science of war, the military student should study the campaigns of great commanders.

"Alexander," says Napoleon, "made eight campaigns; Hannibal, seventeen, one in Spain, fifteen in Italy, and one in Africa; Caesar, thirteen, of which eight were against the Gauls and five against the legions of Pompey; Gustavus Adolphus, three; Turenne, eighteen; Prince Eugene of Savoy, thirteen; Frederick, eleven, in Bohemia, Silesia, and on the banks of the Elbe. The history of these campaigns, written with care, would be a complete treatise on the art of war. From this source the principles which ought to be followed, in offensive as well as in defensive warfare, could at once be obtained."

Again he says:

"Read and meditate upon the wars of the greatest captains. This is the only means of rightly learning the science of war."

Nearly one hundred years ago, (at time of first publication), Napoleon Bonaparte's military achievements amazed the world. Today, when his campaigns and battles are studied by us, their brilliancy and completeness strike us with wonder. The strategy that he exhibited in these campaigns, and the wonderful battle tactics that he employed, strongly impress us with his military greatness. His combinations, his rapid marches, his concentration of masses upon the vital points of his enemy, his victory upon victory, his wonderful power of foreseeing

11

the results of these victories and of appropriating to himself all the advantages to be derived from them, show not merely that he was a genius in war, but that he was the greatest soldier in modern times, and one of the greatest masters of the military art that the world has ever known.

Bonaparte's campaign in Italy in 1796-97, though conducted on a less stupendous scale than many other campaigns in his remarkable career, was surpassed by none in brilliancy, in completeness, in rapidity of movement, and in strategical combinations. Here he first gained his renown as a soldier. Here, at the age of twenty-six, he took the first great step in his immortal career, and. with one small army, in a single campaign, defeated six Austrian armies sent successively against him.

Since Napoleon's time many changes in tactics and in tactical formations have resulted from the inventions of man, from the use of steam, and from discoveries in electricity; but no material changes in strategy have resulted from these causes. Improved weapons and improved methods of transportation may, in some cases, slightly modify strategical movements and strategical combinations; but the principles of strategy, the great principles of war, are the same today as in the days of the great Napoleon. To divide the forces of the enemy and beat them in detail, to manoeuvre upon interior lines, to concentrate an overwhelming mass upon the vital point of the enemy,—these are principles that do not change, however rapid the fire of modern guns, however quick the movements of troops, or however swift the dispatch of orders.

"The application of strategical principles," says Dufour, "is the same at all times and in all places."

To the military student this campaign is, therefore, from a strategical point of view, a very interesting study.

H. H. S.

Fort Bowie, Arizona,
November, 1894.

CHAPTER 1

Montenotte

When in March, 1796, Bonaparte took command of the Army of Italy, he found it in a destitute condition and paralyzed for the want of financial means. He found that many soldiers were without food and sufficient clothing. He addressed the army in these words: "Soldiers, you are naked and ill fed; I will lead you into the most fruitful plains in the world. Rich provinces, great cities, will be in your power. There you will find honour, fame, and wealth."

The situation was as follows. In Northwestern Italy, the Alps on the west and the Apennines on the south divided the opposing forces. To the west and south of these mountain ranges were the French; on the opposite sides, the Austrians and Sardinians. Along the Alps, two armies of about twenty thousand each were holding each other in check. As these two armies neutralized each other during the active operations in the vicinity of the Apennines, they may for the present be omitted from the description of this part of the campaign. Bonaparte's army, known as the Army of Italy, which was about forty thousand strong, and which had only twenty-four cannon of small calibre, extended from Genoa to Nice along the narrow strip of land between the Apennines and the sea.

Upon Bonaparte's right, at Genoa, a British fleet, which was hostile to the French, held possession of the sea. The allied armies on the north side of the Apennines and immediately opposed to Bonaparte, were commanded by Beaulieu, the Austrian general, and consisted of thirty thousand Austrians and twenty thousand Sardinians, the latter under General Colli. They had two hundred cannon. They were facing the passes of Col di Tenda, Ormea, Savona, and Bochetta, which led from their position to that of Bonaparte.

The positions in detail of Bonaparte's forces were as follows. His left was at the pass of Tenda, which was held by seven thousand soldiers; Serrurier's division of seven thousand held the pass of Ormea; Augereau with eight thousand was at Mont San Giacomo; Masséna with eight thousand was at Cadibona; and La Harpe with eight thousand was at Savona, having one of his brigades at Voltri. In the pass of Savona, near Montenotte, works had been constructed and were occupied by the French. On the north side of the Apennines these passes become valleys, and are separated from each other by spurs running out from the main chain. Though these valleys were closed by the fortifications of Coni, Mondovi, and Ceva, which were held by the Sardinians, yet the French divisions, by descending from the passes of the Apennines to the north, could, before arriving at the fortifications, pass from one valley to another over the spurs, and could in this way easily communicate with one another; while on the south side they could still more easily communicate by the Nice-Genoa road.

The allies, who were attempting to guard all the valleys by occupying them all, had their forces greatly subdivided and separated. They held the fortresses and fortified towns of Coni, Mondovi, Ceva, Alessandria, Tortona, Voghera, Turin, and Ivrea. The Sardinians extended from Coni on their right to Millesimo on their left. The Austrians occupied Sassello, Ovada, Voltaggio, Genoa, and the Bochetta pass. The Sardinians were commanded by Colli; the Austrian right or allied centre, by Argenteau; the Austrian left was under the immediate command of Beaulieu, the general in chief of the allied armies.

The line of communication of Bonaparte's army was by the road from Savona to Nice, and thence to its base of operations in France; that of the Austrian army was by two roads,—one through Alessandria and Pavia, and one through Novi and Placentia,—to its base of operations upon the Mincio; that of the Sardinian army was by the roads through Fossano, Cherasco, and Alba, to its base of operations at Turin,

Since the Republic of Genoa, though occupied by the Austrians, was considered neutral territory, Bonaparte asked of the Senate of Genoa permission to conduct his army through Genoa, and thence through the Bochetta pass. Should this permission be granted, his plan was, while holding with small forces the passes of the Apennines, to debouch with his principal army from the Bochetta pass so as to throw his forces upon the Austrians with his front parallel to their communications, and to take in reverse the Sardinians and their fortifications. Should this permission be refused, he expected the Senate to inform Beaulieu of their refusal. In that case he expected the latter to move his forces towards Genoa in anticipation of an attack from that quarter. By so extending his left, Beaulieu would still more scatter his forces and weaken his centre, and thus give Bonaparte an opportunity to throw his masses upon this isolated centre, defeat it, and separate the allies.

On the other hand, Beaulieu, who had probably heard of Bonaparte's request and of the extension of his right wing to Voltri, was expecting an attack in force by way of Genoa. He resolved to anticipate this movement. His plan was to meet it by moving his left wing through Genoa to attack Bonaparte in front, while his centre, commanded by Argenteau, was to advance upon Savona, cut off the French right wing from its communications, and together they were to capture this wing, or envelop it and drive it into the sea. By adopting this plan, he expected an additional advantage; namely, that of establishing communication with Nelson, who was in the waters of Genoa with an English squadron.

Such was the situation of the opposing forces, and such were the plans of the two commanders, when, on April 10th, Beaulieu began active operations. He moved his left, about one third of his entire army, through the Bochetta pass upon Genoa and Voltri; and ordered his centre, consisting of ten thousand men under Argenteau, to move at the same time from Sassello upon Savona, Beaulieu reached Voltri the next day, and made two unsuccessful attacks upon the brigade there. Argenteau was also unsuccessful; he was stopped on the 11th by the works in the pass near Montenotte; for though these works were defended by only twelve hundred men, and though he attacked with great fury all day, he did not succeed in carrying the position.

On the 11th of April, while these two small forces—the brigade at Voltri and the twelve hundred men in the pass—were engaged with superior numbers, Bonaparte was active in making preparations to crush Argenteau. He gave orders to his division commanders as follows: Masséna was to leave Cadibona, march to Cairo, then cross the ridge towards Argenteau and be ready to fall on his flank and rear; Augereau, to march from San Giacomo to Cairo and be ready to hold back the Sardinians; La Harpe, to recall his brigade from Voltri, then march with his whole division to the pass near Montenotte and post it behind the works there. During the day and night of the 11th, these movements were all successfully accomplished; and on the morning of, the 12th Bonaparte directed La Harpe to attack Argenteau in front, and Masséna to attack him on the flank and rear. Argenteau was defeated. His army was routed, and the remnants and stragglers rallied at Dego.

.By this battle, known as Montenotte, the centre of the allies was broken. The first step in Bonaparte's plan had been accomplished. Beaulieu was still south of the Apennines. He advanced from Voltri, but, finding no enemy and hearing the guns of Montenotte, he halted for information; and on the morning of April 13th, having learned of the defeat of his centre, he faced about his own columns and ordered them to concentrate at Dego.

While Beaulieu was retracing his steps, Bonaparte was preparing to attack the left of the Sardinians, who were divided into two armies. One, under Colli, was at Ceva; and the other, under Provera, at Millesimo. Bonaparte ordered La Harpe to Sassello to hold back any Austrians in that direction, and ordered Serrurier to make false attacks from Ormea to Ceva against Colli, so as to keep him occupied and prevent his re-enforcing Provera. Then, at the head of Masséna's and Augereau's divisions, he marched against Provera at Millesimo, defeated him, and. on the morning of the 14th captured his army.

On the same day, Bonaparte, leaving Augereau in front of Colli to aid Serrurier, conducted the divisions of La Harpe and Masséna upon Dego, drove back and defeated the Austrians there, and also defeated, the next day, a corps of Beaulieu's army that was attempting to reach Dego. Beaulieu, learning of Bonaparte's success at Dego, now attempted to concentrate his scattered troops at Acqui.

Thus in four days Bonaparte had crushed the centre of the allies, captured a Sardinian army upon his left, and forced back the Austrians threatening his right. Now, with his divisions perched upon the spurs of the Apennines, with his whole army in a central position and his right well extended between the wings of the allies, he was preparing to move against the Sardinians, to crush them if he could, or to drive them back upon Turin and detach them from the alliance, so as to leave himself free to meet the Austrians single-handed upon the fertile plains of Northern Italy. Accordingly, he ordered La Harpe to San Benedetto to watch Beaulieu, and either to protect the French rear should the Austrians move by Cairo, or to prevent the junction of Beaulieu with Colli by way of Alba; he also ordered a brigade to remain at Cairo in order to protect the French communications with Savona.

These dispositions having been made, Bonaparte with Masséna's,

Augereau's, and Serrurier's divisions attacked the Sardinians at Ceva and Mondovi, and drove them towards Turin. The Austrians attempted to join the Sardinians at Alba; but Bonaparte united his divisions there, and thus destroyed Beaulieu's last hope of a junction with his ally. The French continued their advance on Turin. The Sardinians then treated separately for peace, and gave up to the French the fortresses of Alessandria, Coni, Tortona, and the citadel of Ceva.

By these manoeuvres, Bonaparte's lines of communication with Nice by the passes of Savona, Ormea, and Tenda, and directly with France by the much shorter route of Mont Cenis, were secured.

Thus it appears that Bonaparte made his first movement against the allies on April 11th; and that the armistice of Cherasco was signed with the Sardinians on April 28th. In eighteen days he had turned the Apennines, driven back the allies, won six victories captured or killed more than twelve thousand men, taken more than forty cannon, detached the Sardinians from the Austrians, compelled the former to make a separate peace, and had acquired, as a base for future operations against the Austrians, the three fortresses of Coni, Tortona, and Alessandria, with their artillery, magazines, and stores.

COMMENTS

For a proper concentration for battle, not taking into account obstacles such as mountains, rivers, and fortifications, the front; of an army of one hundred and fifty thousand men or less should not be more than thirty miles. However, in this case it is to be noticed that both armies, at the outset, had much longer fronts,—that of the French extending from Tenda to Savona, a distance of about fifty miles; that of the allies, from Coni to Voltaggio, about seventy-five miles. But the Apennines, which were intervening obstacles, were favourable to Bonaparte, who could with small forces easily hold the passes, and could quickly concentrate his army at any point upon his front by the road south of them. During this concentration, his forces would be perfectly protected by the mountains from the attacks of the allies. The Apennines, therefore, allowed him to extend his front with safety beyond thirty miles.

On the other hand, the allies were not only more extended than the French, but they had their principal forces at the ends of their long line. Furthermore, these forces themselves were separated into parts by the spurs of the Apennines, which made it difficult to re-enforce any portion of their front without the danger of being struck in flank by

SWISS ALPS
Mont Cenis
Turin
SARDINIA
Alessandria
Marengo
Tortona
Voghera
Novi
Acqui
Cherasco
Genoa
Savona
Cairo
APENNINES
Col di Tenda
GULF OF GENOA
LIGURIAN
Milan
Nice

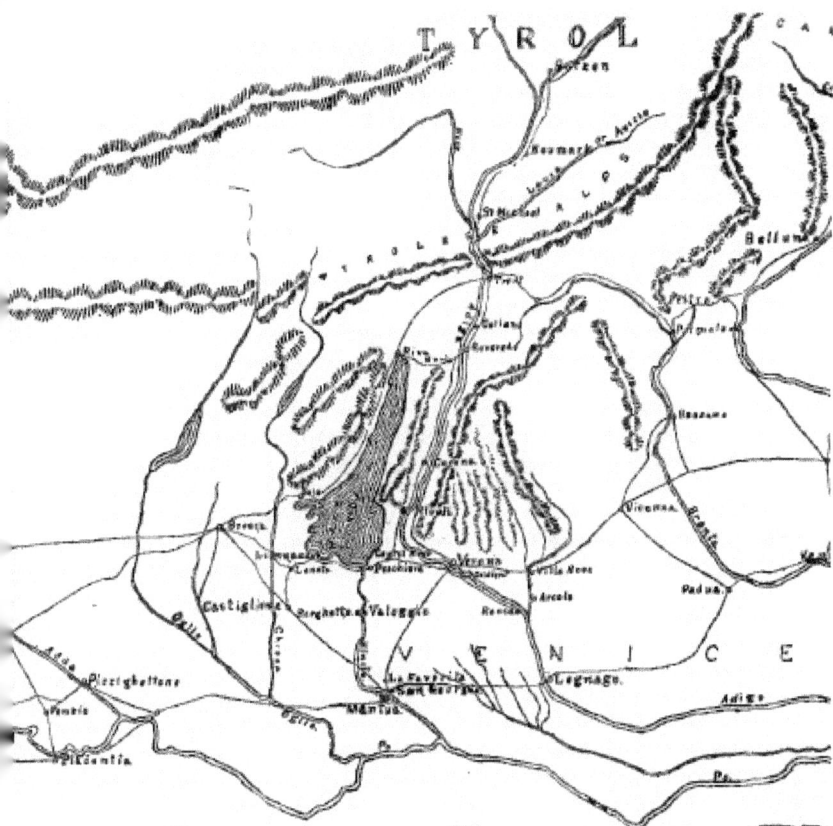
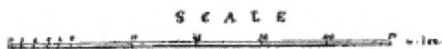

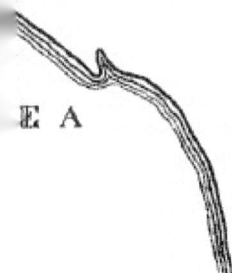

FIRST PART OF CAMPAIGN

Bonaparte's divisions issuing from the passes of the Apennines. Upon the principle that "an army in motion should always be able to concentrate for battle within a single day," it is safe to say that the front of the allies should not have been longer than thirty miles. But it was more than twice this distance; they had scattered their forces; they had weakened their line in proportion as they had extended it, and had thus allowed their adversary to break through and divide their army, so as to force them to choose between retreating, and fighting with only a part of their forces.

Why did the Austrian general so scatter his forces? Why did he make this fatal mistake? At this time, and also in after years, the Austrian generals, in making war, seemed to believe in a division of forces. They made war by detachments. Their main army was invariably divided into two or three armies, and these were often subdivided. Under this system they expected to hold all the parts of their front by occupying them all. But there was another reason for the separation of the Austrian and Sardinian armies. Beaulieu was anxious about his lines of communication, and in order to protect them he separated his forces.

This anxiety, even though it led to error, was natural; for the lines of communication of an army are always of the utmost importance to its safety. In every manoeuvre, combination, and battle of a campaign, the commanding general should give the most careful consideration to his communications,—to their direction, extent, and protection. In order to fight, soldiers must have food and ammunition. The loss of an army's communications almost always leads to immediate disaster.

"While the distant spectator," says Hamley, "imagines a general to be intent only on striking or parrying a blow, he probably directs a hundred glances, a hundred anxious thoughts, to the communications in his rear, for one that he bestows upon his adversary's front."

Now, the Sardinians at Ceva and Millesimo directly covered their communications with Turin. The Austrians at Ovada and Voltaggio covered their communications back through Pavia to their base on the Mincio. Beaulieu, being anxious about his communications, had therefore divided his forces; and as they fell back along these divergent lines of communication, they of necessity became more and more separated. That it was an error to attempt, by separating these two armies, to cover directly their communications, is shown by the victor.

20

Napoleon himself, in his criticism of the allies' position. He says:—

"But the army under the orders of Colli, instead of moving upon Millesimo, should have supported itself upon Dego. It was an error to suppose that, in order to cover Turin, Colli must station himself directly upon the road to that city. The united armies at Dego would have covered Milan, because they would have been astride of the high road of Montferrat; they would have covered Turin, because they would have been near the road to that place. United, the two forces would have been superior to the French army; separated, they were lost."

Though the disposition of the forces of the Austrian commander-in-chief were faulty in so many- particulars, it is interesting to note how very near he came to being successful. Had his centre, under Argenteau, succeeded in the assaults of the earthworks in Savona pass, the Army of Italy, instead of the allies, might have been cut in two. By means of these works, a handful of men were enabled to repulse the furious assaults of many times their number, and thus give to Bonaparte time to make his dispositions for the destruction of Argenteau.

Though these insignificant works played for a few hours an important part in the campaign, it is worthy of notice that the strong fortresses which were held by the allies, and which were on the direct line of Bonaparte's operations, did not stop his advance for a moment; even though, on account of having no siege artillery and only a few cannon of small calibre, he could not completely invest them. He pushed forward past them to decide, if possible, their fate upon the open battlefield. "It is upon the open field of battle," said Napoleon thirteen years afterwards, "that the fate of fortresses and empires is decided."

As soon as Beaulieu learned of the defeat of his centre, he turned back for fear of losing his own communications, and to avoid meeting single-handed Bonaparte's victorious army. Upon this point, Hamley comments as follows:—

Upon the defeat of Argenteau at Montenotte, Beaulieu was compelled to pause. For though he was prepared to attack the French in front of him, yet it was on the assumption that Argenteau would co-operate by an attack on their flank and rear; and this was only possible on condition that the French should be concentrating towards Voltri. Therefore, when Beaulieu found that they had retired from that point, he knew they must be either beyond the reach of Argenteau, by retreating westward beyond Savona,—in which case he would presently be apprised of it by the advance-guard of his colleague issuing from the pass,—or that they had concentrated for an attack, in which case he might, if he should advance, find himself single-handed in the presence of a victorious enemy, as would indeed have been the case. Therefore, as soon as he was certified of disaster to his colleague, he hastened to recover his communications, which he might else find to be endangered.

Thus far we have said nothing about the French and Sardinian armies in the Alps, for the reason that they neutralized each other, and had no immediate effect upon the results. It will now be noticed, that, when Bonaparte was advancing upon Turin, both of the Sardinian armies were between him and Kellerman, the commander of the French army in the Alps. The Sardinian general could, therefore, have left a small containing force [1] before Kellerman and have massed against Bonaparte, thus playing the same game against him that he had played against Beaulieu. Upon this point Hamley says:—

It was to guard against such a contingency that Bonaparte, on the 25th, from Fossano pressed the commander of the right of Kellerman's army to issue from the Alps towards him. But it is to be observed, first, that, even when thus combined, the Sardinians would have been inferior to Bonaparte in numbers, having been only equal to his single army at the outset; and, secondly, that the distance from Mont Cenis to Turin is so short that Kellerman, unless strongly opposed, might reach in a single march and enclose their armies while he seized their capital.

The Sardinians fought hard. Before they treated for peace, they were defeated in several battles. This was due in a great measure to the plan of campaign which Bonaparte adopted. When he threw his forces against the Sardinians, they fell back after each battle upon their communications with Turin, rallied their scattered troops, and were ready in a short time to fight again. Had Bonaparte held the passes of the Apennines with small forces, issued with his principal army from the Bochetta pass with his front parallel to the Austrian communications, and attacked successfully, he would in all probability have decided the campaign in a single battle; for a defeat of the Austrian army, or of both armies combined, meant a loss of the Austrian communications,—in other words, meant ruin to the Austrian army. Had the Austrians alone

---

1. "Containing force. A body of troops charged with the duty of holding in check a body (generally numerically superior) of the enemy, while the main efforts of the army are directed against another portion of the hostile forces."—Wagner.

been defeated, the Sardinians would hardly have been able, single-handed, to cope successfully with Bonaparte, and would in all probability have treated for peace. Under circumstances very similar to this supposititious case, Bonaparte, in the Marengo campaign, debouched from the St Bernard pass, threw his army from the north upon these same Austrian communications, and in one battle decided the fate of the whole Austrian army.

But there were several reasons for not adopting this plan besides the one already given. First: Beaulieu was expecting an attack in force from Bonaparte's right, and was prepared for it. Second: The allies by extending their front had weakened and isolated their centre. Third: An attack by the right must necessarily cause a concentration of the allies, and this was the very thing that Bonaparte wished to prevent. Fourth: Besides these military reasons, there was also a political one, which appears in the instructions given to Bonaparte by the Directory, as follows:

The Austrians, as was shown in the last campaign, trouble themselves very little about the disaster of the allies, and, in moments of danger, far from seeking effectually to protect them, immediately separate from them and are concerned only to cover the country which belongs to themselves.

This fact, taken in connection with the fact that the lines of communication of the two armies back to their bases of operation were divergent, was another strong reason for striking at the centre and separating the allies. Fifth: If Bonaparte really had any serious doubts as to which was the better plan of campaign, the offensive movement in force by Beaulieu upon Genoa and Voltri decided the question in favour of an attack upon the centre. Beaulieu's movement was a fatal one; by it he extended still more his front, separated himself more and more from Argenteau, and, by his fruitless march against an almost imaginary enemy, took from the field of action one third of his entire army. When Bonaparte saw this, he immediately took advantage of it, and struck with the rapidity of lightning. In four days he gained four victories. Before Beaulieu's return, Montenotte, Millesimo, and the two battles of Dego had been fought and won.

Operating upon interior lines from his central position, Bonaparte could concentrate his divisions much more rapidly than the enemy, who was operating upon exterior or double lines. During these actions, with one division, sometimes two, as a containing force, he held back a portion of the allies, and then concentrated an overwhelming mass upon their remaining forces at some decisive point. Though the allies outnumbered him, yet he invariably brought a superior force against them upon the battlefield. At Montenotte, La Harpe and Masséna had sixteen thousand, Argenteau only ten thousand; at Millesimo, Masséna and Augereau had nearly sixteen thousand, Provera several thousand less; at Dego, La Harpe and Masséna engaged about six thousand Austrian soldiers, and the next day about six thousand more; at Mondovi, Bonaparte had three divisions—Serrurier's, Augereau's, and Masséna's—for an attack against the remnant of the Sardinian army, about eight thousand strong. So to manoeuvre as to divide the forces of the enemy and beat them in detail, so to manoeuvre as always to bring an overwhelming mass upon the vital point of the enemy, so to manoeuvre with forty thousand soldiers against fifty thousand as to outnumber the enemy upon every battlefield,—this is generalship, this is strategy; it is more, it is victory. Victory is the aim of all strategy.

This much of the campaign, Bonaparte's first, was very similar to the Waterloo campaign, his last. In the first, he was opposed by the Sardinians and Austrians; in the last, by the English and the Prussians. In each case, the armies opposed to him had divergent lines of communication. In each case, he used his own army as an entering wedge to separate the allies; and when, after defeating the Prussians, he detached a containing force to hold them in check while he massed his force against the English, he was repeating the manoeuvre that nineteen years before had made him victorious in the beginning of his matchless military career.

CHAPTER 2

Lodi

Before entering upon a detailed description of this part of the campaign, it will be well to describe in a few words the nature of the country in which the French and Austrians during the remainder of the year 1796 conducted their operations; and also to point out the sources from which both sides obtained supplies for their men and animals.

Northern Italy was the theatre of war.[1] Between the Tyrolese Alps, in the extreme northern part of Italy, and the Ligurian and Adriatic Seas, the country is fertile and the climate mild. The rivers Sesia, Ticino, Adda, Oglio, and Chiesa run south-eastward from the Alpine region of the north and join the Po, which, running eastward through most of its course, collects their waters into one body and pours them into the Gulf of Venice. The Mincio, which is the outlet of Lake Garda, flows south to the fortress of Mantua, at this time held by the Austrians, and then flows southeast into the Po. The Adige, which is deep and unfordable, flows south along the east side of Lake Garda till opposite the south end of the lake, and then southeast into the Gulf of Venice.

Up on the east bank of this river, at the point where the mountains end and the plains begin, is the fortified town of Verona; and on the same bank, thirty miles nearer the mouth, is the fortified town of Legnago. The Brenta rises in the Tyrol near Trent, and flows southeast, past the town of Bassano and near the town of Padua, into the Gulf of

---

1. "The theatre of war comprises all the territory upon which the parties may assail each other, whether it belongs to themselves, to their allies, or to weaker states who may be drawn into the war through fear or interest. . . . The theatre of war may thus be undefined, and must not be confounded with the theatre of operations of one or the other army."—Jomini.

Venice. Along the line of the Alps are a number of lakes. The largest of these is Garda, which is thirty miles long and two to eight miles wide. Its northern end extends well into the mountains; its southern end, into the plains of Italy.

In this well-watered and fertile country, Bonaparte found supplies in abundance for his army. When he took command of the Army of Italy, his soldiers were suffering for the necessaries of life. Upon the barren rocks of the Apennines nothing would grow. The bread and wine necessary to hold body and soul together came mostly from France. But as soon as his soldiers descended the mountains into the fertile plains of Italy they found plenty of food for themselves and plenty of forage for their animals. By levying contributions upon the invaded territory Bonaparte collected these supplies. Thus from the very start he made war support war. Money, clothing, food, forage, wine,—in fact all the supplies needed for his army except ammunition, which came from France,—were obtained from the invaded and conquered territory. With the money and supplies thus obtained, he established in Italy magazines and hospitals, which, with the fortresses he had already acquired, formed a secondary base of operations for the further prosecution of the war.

The Austrians obtained their ammunition from Austria and their supplies from Italy; but as soon as they were pushed back into the Alps, they were compelled to obtain the greater portion of their supplies also from Austria.

The situations of the opposing forces were, therefore, in many respects similar. Behind the French army were the Apennines and French Alps; behind the Austrian army were the Tyrolese and Swiss Alps. As each army advanced into the valley of the Po, supplies were obtained in abundance; as each fell back into the mountains, supplies were obtained with difficulty. These facts should be kept in mind by the reader that he may understand thoroughly the succeeding movements.

The Sardinians, having been defeated by Bonaparte, had, by the armistice of Cherasco, left him free to proceed against the Austrian army. Bonaparte with about forty thousand soldiers was at Alessandria. Beaulieu with about thirty thousand was occupying Valeggio, and had in addition twelve thousand at Mantua.

The French lines of communication extended from Alessandria, through the passes of the Alps and the Apennines, into France. The Austrian lines of communication extended through Milan and Pavia, around the south end of Lake Garda, and thence along the high-road to Austria, which penetrates the Tyrol by the valley of the Upper Adige.

Bonaparte, by causing to be inserted in the armistice of Cherasco a stipulation that he should be allowed to cross the Po at Valenza, and by moving his troops towards that place, had led the Austrian commander to expect him there. But he did not intend to cross at that point. On May 6th he took his cavalry, three thousand five hundred grenadiers, and twenty-four pieces of cannon, as an advance-guard, and marched rapidly down the Po to Placentia. In thirty-six hours he marched forty miles. His main army followed him in *echelon* by divisions.

At Placentia he forced a crossing, but, having no pontoon train, he had to build a bridge for the passage of the main army, and on this account his divisions were considerably delayed. He advanced with what force he had, attacked the Austrians at Fombio, defeated them, and drove them before him. Expecting to find the Austrian main force between the Ticino and the Adda, he stationed one division on the Lower Adda to protect his right, and one at Pavia to protect his left, while with his main force he ascended the Adda towards Milan. Upon his arrival at Lodi, he found that Beaulieu, having crossed the Adda with his main army, had made good his escape; but that he had left a force of twelve thousand at the bridge of Lodi to defend it. This force was the Austrian rear-guard. Bonaparte formed his grenadiers, ordered an attack, and, with Lannes and himself at the head of the attacking column, carried the bridge after a desperate fight and a great loss of life on both sides. The Austrians retreated behind the Mincio, and there halted in a strong position, with Lake Garda on their right and Mantua on their left.

Bonaparte with his victorious columns then made a triumphal march into Milan, which he entered just one month and three days after the Battle of Montenotte. But he did not remain there long. After investing the citadel of Milan, in which Beaulieu had left a garrison of two thousand Austrians, Bonaparte hastened with his main army to the Mincio to drive the Austrians out of Italy. His purpose was to attack the Austrian centre at Borghetto. In order to deceive the Austrians as to the real point of attack, he caused a demonstration to be made against Peschiera. Then, on May 29th, he hurled his cavalry under Murat upon Borghetto. He supported it with artillery and infantry. The French were victorious. They carried the bridge there, broke through the Austrian line, drove the Austrian army into the Tyrol, and separated this army from Mantua with its twelve thousand combatants. *The first Austrian army was defeated.*

Bonaparte now marched to the Adige, took possession of Verona and Legnago, and on June 14th began the investment of Mantua.

COMMENTS

When Bonaparte crossed the Po at Placentia, he expected to throw his whole army upon the Austrian communications, to envelop their army, and compel its surrender; but, having no pontoon train, he was delayed at the crossing, and this delay gave to Beaulieu the opportunity to make his escape.

"If I had had a good pontoon equipage," said Bonaparte, speaking of this passage of the Po, "the fate of the enemy's army had been sealed."

And, judging from what in after years he accomplished at Marengo and Ulm, where, by manoeuvres similar to this, he threw his army upon his enemies' communications, we cannot avoid the belief that, had it not been for the delay, he would have here captured the entire Austrian army.

If he had attempted to cross, or had crossed, the Po at Valenza, as he had purposely made the Austrians believe he would do, the two armies would have been facing each other with their lines of communication (and, in this case, their lines of retreat) perpendicular to their fronts. In this situation, the advantages of victory and the disadvantages of defeat would have been the same or nearly so to each of the two armies. Neither would have had the advantage in position, and in case of defeat either could have retreated with little or no danger of losing its communications. But it was to avoid this, and to give the advantage to the French, that Bonaparte made his flank movement. For this reason he placed his army on the north side of the Po with his front parallel to the Austrian communications.

In this position, the Austrians, in order to give battle, must form front to a flank,[2] and if defeated must lose their communications. On the other hand, the French if defeated could fall back across the Po with little or no danger of losing their communications.

In the march down the Po to gain this position upon the Austrian flank, the French army had of necessity to expose its own flank to the enemy. The river, however, in a measure protected the French from a flank attack; but Bonaparte took further precautions: he marched

---

2. An army *forms front to a flank* when it operates on a front parallel to the line communicating with its base.

rapidly, and required his divisions to march in *echelon* with the leading division farthest from the river. By this means they supported one another, and, in case the leading division had been attacked in flank, the rear divisions could in turn have struck the Austrians in flank- When Bonaparte arrived before Lodi, Beaulieu had already crossed the Adda with his main army. The Austrian force at Lodi was simply Beaulieu's rear-guard, which he had left there to protect his retreat. For these reasons, Bonaparte's victory there had but little effect upon the result of the campaign. From a strategical point of view, therefore, the battle at the bridge of Lodi was unimportant. Nevertheless, it gave to Bonaparte the opportunity to show his soldiers that he himself was brave and fearless, and it covered Lannes with glory. Jomini, writing of this battle in his *Life of Napoleon*, puts into Bonaparte's mouth these words:

> The occasion furnished an opportunity for stamping by some bold stroke the character of my individual actions, and I did not let it escape. The affair might be attended with the loss of a few hundred men; but even should I be defeated, it could not have the least influence on the result of the campaign. . . . This was merely an affair of a rear-guard, but still it was a brilliant one.

On April 11th, Bonaparte made his first movement against the Sardinians and Austrians from the narrow strip of land between the Apennines and the sea. On May 29th, he crushed the Austrians at Borghetto, and drove them into the Tyrol. In less than two months, he had compelled the Sardinians to make peace, and had driven the Austrians out of Italy. Could he hold Italy? This was now the problem.

CHAPTER 3

Lonato and Castiglione

Austria became alarmed at Bonaparte's progress. She determined to make a great effort for the relief of Mantua and for the recovery of Italy. The Austrian army in the Tyrol was increased to sixty thousand men. Marshal Wurmser, an old man, but a brave Soldier, who had distinguished himself in several Austrian campaigns, received the command of this army. Besides these sixty thousand there were twelve thousand Austrian soldiers shut up in Mantua.

Bonaparte had altogether forty-five thousand soldiers. Serrurier's division, ten thousand strong, was besieging Mantua; Augereau with eight thousand was at Legnago; Masséna with fifteen thousand was at Verona and Rivoli; Sauret with four thousand was at Salo; and in the rear of these divisions about eight thousand were in reserve.

From Trent, where the Austrian army was assembled, three direct routes led to Bonaparte's position. One route was by the road from Trent to Riva, and thence along the west side of Lake Garda to Brescia. This road, which passed through a mountainous country, was impassable for artillery. The other two routes were by the two roads from Roveredo down the Adige,—one to Rivoli by the right bank of the river, and the other to Verona by the left bank. These two roads were passable for artillery.

Marshal Wurmser divided his forces into two armies: one, twenty-five thousand strong, commanded by Quasdanovich, marched on the west side of Lake Garda; the other, thirty-five thousand strong, commanded by Wurmser himself, descended the Adige in two columns, one on each side of the river. His plan was to have these two columns make simultaneous attacks upon Rivoli and Verona, and, while these attacks were being made, he expected Quasdanovich to debouch by Salo on the French line of communications. In this way Wurmser expected to envelop and capture the whole French army.

Bonaparte, not being strong enough to take the offensive, had no plan. He was waiting for developments. On July 30th he learned that the Austrians were advancing on both sides of the lake. He learned that Masséna had been driven back from Rivoli, and that Sauret had been driven back from Salo. Already the Austrians were debouching on his rear; in a few hours at most they would sever his communications. His situation was critical and time was precious. He hastily called a council of war. All his generals except Augereau advised retreat; but nevertheless Bonaparte decided to fight, and immediately formed his plan. It was to raise the siege of Mantua and to concentrate at once all his available force at the lower end of Lake Garda, where, from his central position, he could fall with almost his entire force on one and then on the other of the two Austrian armies. By this means he hoped to defeat them separately, and to prevent them from uniting on the Mincio.

On the same day that the council of war was assembled, Bonaparte gave his orders to his division commanders. The next day, July 31st, was a day of concentration. Masséna fell back across the Mincio. Augereau left Legnago and marched to join Masséna. At the crossings of the Mincio, both division commanders left rear-guards to watch the march of the enemy. On the same day Serrurier raised the siege of Mantua, spiked his guns, burned his carriages, buried his projectiles, and began his march to join Masséna and Augereau. Meanwhile, Wurmser, having united his two columns, was approaching the Mincio. On the afternoon of the same day, and on the next day, Bonaparte with Masséna's and Augereau's divisions attacked and worsted Quasdanovich at Lonato, Brescia, and Salo, without doing him a great amount of damage.

On August 1st Bonaparte halted on the Chiesa. He had succeeded in placing Masséna's and Augereau's divisions between Wurmser and Quasdanovich. He had forced back the latter into the mountains upon the west side of Lake Garda; and, having advanced to the Chiesa, he found that his communications with Milan were safe. In order still to maintain his central position, and to be ready to meet Wurmser, whom he was expecting from the direction of the Mincio, he turned back his columns and marched towards Lonato and Castiglione. During these manoeuvres, Wurmser Crossed the Mincio and directed one of his divisions on Lonato and one on Castiglione, but with the main part of his army continued his march on Mantua. Meanwhile, Quasdanovich, having seen the necessity of uniting with Wurmser, was extending his left towards Lonato.

On August 2nd Bonaparte, having received a part of Serrurier's division, directed Masséna upon Lonato, and Augereau Upon Castiglione. On the same day, Wurmser arrived at Mantua, revictualled the garrison, and then marched out in the direction of Castiglione to find Bonaparte.

On August 3rd Masséna fought the Battle of Lonato, and Augereau fought the Battle of Castiglione. After hard fighting both were victorious. Quasdanovich was pursued and badly cut up. He retreated on Riva.

Bonaparte, having disposed of Quasdanovich, now turned his attention to Wurmser, who was marching on Castiglione, On August 4th he ordered all his available force to concentrate at this place, and on August 5th he fought the second Battle of Castiglione. Masséna and Augereau attacked Wurmser in front, while Serrurier attacked his left flank. Wurmser was beaten and driven across the Mincio. Bonaparte followed up his victory, attacked again at Peschiera, and drove the Austrians into the Tyrol. *The second Austrian army was defeated.* The French divisions were again established on the Adige, and Mantua was again invested. In six days Bonaparte had captured, killed, or wounded nearly twenty thousand Austrians, and lost but seven thousand French. In six days he had fought and won three pitched battles, had almost annihilated Wurmser's army, and had for the second time driven the Austrians out of Italy.

COMMENTS

In this part of the campaign, sixty thousand Austrians were marching down upon Bonaparte, and twelve thousand in Mantua were in his rear; yet with only forty-five thousand soldiers he succeeded in winning every battle and in utterly routing the Austrian forces. How did he accomplish this? It was not that the Austrians lacked courage; for they are a brave people, and fought hard, even desperately. How, then, did he win such success? The answer is, that he won it by his marches, by his concentrations for battle, by utilising every available French soldier, by bringing upon every battlefield a stronger force than his adversary, and by taking advantage of the errors made by the Austrian commander.

In advancing upon the French on both sides of Lake Garda, Wurmser committed a great error. With Lake Garda separating his two armies, neither could support the other. This error allowed Bonaparte to place almost his entire force at the foot of the lake, where he could bring a superior force against either army. To separate the forces of his enemy at the beginning of a campaign was one of Bonaparte's first, endeavours. It was one of his master strokes. In order to separate his enemy's forces, he had, at the beginning of his career in Italy, fought the battle of Montenotte. But in the case before us no battle was necessary to accomplish this object. Wurmser, by separating his forces, did the very thing that Bonaparte wished him to do. It is remarkable that Wurmser should have made this movement; for he certainly knew that Bonaparte's success in the Montenotte campaign had been gained against the Austrians and Sardinians by overwhelming the centre of the allied armies, by separating them and keeping them separated till, by concentrating a superior force against one and then the other, he had succeeded in defeating both.

In advancing on the east side of Lake Garda in two columns separated by the river Adige, Wurmser committed another error. These two columns, by following the two roads down the Adige, one to Rivoli and the other to Verona, were, as they approached these places, separated by an unfordable river and by impassable mountains. But the French, who were occupying both places, had easy communication between them by the bridge over the Adige at Verona. Thus it is seen how a small containing force could have checked the advance of one column, while a concentration was being made against the other. Such a plan surely offered great chances of victory to Bonaparte. Other considerations, however, which will be discussed later, led him to adopt a different plan.

In going to relieve Mantua before he had defeated the French army, Wurmser made a third great error. While Bonaparte was hotly engaged with Quasdanovich, Wurmser was making a fruitless march into, Mantua. Had he crossed the Mincio and connected with Quasdanovich a day or so before the battles of Lonato and Castiglione, and brought upon these battlefields, thirty thousand fresh troops, as he could easily have done, Bonaparte would probably have been defeated. Here, Wurmser had the opportunity of rectifying his errors; but, instead of doing so, he continued still to blunder on with that persistency in error that seemed to follow nearly all the Austrian commanders throughout the campaign.

It is, however, very easy to criticise Wurmser after the event; but it was not so easy for him to see clearly at the time what to do. Being anxious to relieve Mantua, he needed but the opportunity. His soldiers there, were in a critical condition and needed supplies. This fact undoubtedly made a strong impression on his mind. To the accomplishment of the relief of Mantua everything seemed favourable; for, when he reached Rivoli, Masséna retreated towards Milan; Augereau, too, marched towards Milan and crossed the Mincio; and even Serrurier, after raising the siege of Mantua, marched in the same direction. Knowing all this, Wurmser thought the French were retreating on Milan. He therefore concluded that he would revictual Mantua before starting in pursuit of Bonaparte. This conclusion was a very natural one; still he should have known that Bonaparte would not yield Italy without a battle; he should have known that the victor of Montenotte, of Dego, of Mondovi, of Millesimo, and of Lodi would not seek safety in retreat without at least making one great effort to hold what he had conquered.

Napoleon has passed judgement upon this part of the campaign as follows:—

> Wurmser's plan was defective; his three corps were separated by two large rivers (the Adige and the Mincio), several mountain chains, and Lake Garda. He ought either to have debouched with all his forces between Lake Garda and the Adige, or to have advanced with his united army by the Chiesa upon Brescia. In the execution of his plan, he committed an error which cost him dear: he wasted two days in marching to Mantua. He should, on the contrary, have thrown two bridges over the Mincio at Peschiera, hastily crossed this river, joined his right at Lonato, Desenzano, and Salo, and thus, by rapidly uniting his divided, forces, have repaired the defects of his plan.

While Wurmser was marching and counter-marching with half of his command to no purpose, Bonaparte was taking advantage of every moment of time, and using every one of his available men. At no time does Wurmser bring half of his force upon the battlefield, while on August 3rd and on August 5th Bonaparte concentrates there nearly the whole of his army. *By a superiority of force upon the battlefields, he won these victories.* The energy that he infused into this part of the campaign is something wonderful. On July 30th he learned that the French were being driven back on both sides of Lake Garda.

On the same day he called a council of war and then issued his orders. In the next twenty-four hours he concentrated for battle, drove back the Austrians from Desenzano and Salo, and recovered his communications. For six days he was fighting almost constantly. With the rapidity of lightning he struck blow after blow. Though he had but a handful of men, his grenadiers seemed to be everywhere. They were always in the right place at the right time. They marched by night and fought by day. He himself was everywhere, tireless and indomitable.

"In a few days," says Thiers, "he had killed five horses; he would not intrust any one with the execution of his orders; he was determined to see everything, to verify everything, to animate all by his presence."

In order to understand this Lonato-Castiglione part of the campaign from a strategical point of view, let us notice the positions of all the forces on July 29th, the day before Bonaparte decided to concentrate.

The Austrian right wing, twenty-five thousand strong, was before Salo; the Austrian centre, eighteen thousand strong, before Rivoli; the Austrian left wing, seventeen thousand strong, before Verona; and twelve thousand were at Mantua.

The French left wing, four thousand strong, commanded by Sauret, was at Salo; their centre, fifteen thousand strong, commanded by Masséna, was at Verona and Rivoli; their right, eight thousand strong, commanded by Augereau, was at Legnago; about eight thousand were in reserve; and Serrurier had ten thousand before Mantua.

The time had arrived when Bonaparte had either to retreat or to fight. He decided to fight. He could adopt any one of the following plans: he could fall back with all his forces and cover Mantua; or he could concentrate against the Austrian left wing at Verona, or against the Austrian centre at Rivoli, or against the Austrian right at Lonato. Let us examine each one of these plans in the order named, that we may see which one would probably have procured him the greatest advantages.

First: Had he fallen back from his position on the Adige to cover Mantua, he could not have taken advantage of the errors that Wurmser had made in separating his columns by impassable obstacles; for as soon as the Austrian armies in their advance had passed Verona, Rivoli, and Lake Garda, there would have been no further obstacles to prevent their uniting against Bonaparte. In this case he would have had the whole Austrian army in his front, and twelve thousand in his rear. As ten thousand of his own soldiers were necessary to bold Mantua, he would have had but thirty-five thousand Frenchmen with whom to oppose sixty thousand Austrians.

Second: Had he made his principal attack at Verona, he would have concentrated near that place and would have crossed the Adige with the greater part of his forces. Undoubtedly he would have been victorious against the Austrian left; but as he had only sufficient force to act offensively; against one column at a time, the Austrian right and centre, consisting of forty-three thousand soldiers, and the garrison at Mantua, consisting of twelve thousand, could meanwhile have united upon his rear. Such a movement would have cut off his retreat on Milan, and would have led, in all probability, to the annihilation of his army.

Third: There are several strong reasons why the concentrated attack upon the Austrians should have been made at Rivoli. The French army could have been united near there just as easily as at Mantua, Verona, or Lonato. A concentrated attack there would have hopelessly separated the other two Austrian columns. As Verona was a fortified town, a small force could have easily held the place for a few days, which would have given sufficient time for a concentration and attack at Rivoli. And, besides, as a battlefield Rivoli offered many advantages to Bonaparte. It was here that, a few months afterwards, he fought and won, with inferior forces, a great battle,—one of the greatest tactical battles mentioned in history.

Let us suppose that Bonaparte, had chosen to attack the Austrians at Rivoli, and had issued orders as follows: the reserve to march on Rivoli; Augereau to leave two thousand soldiers at Legnago and to ascend the south bank of the Adige towards Rivoli; Masséna to withdraw all his force from Verona, except four thousand to hold the town, and to march to Rivoli; Serrurier to raise the siege of Mantua, to guard the crossings of the Mincio with part of his. division, and with the other part to fall back on Peschiera; Sauret to fall back on Peschiera, to remain there till relieved by Serrurier, and then to join Bonaparte at Rivoli. In twenty-four hours, Bonaparte could in this way have concentrated twenty-nine, thousand soldiers with whom, to attack the Austrian centre, eighteen thousand strong.

Then, by transferring this army to Verona, he could have had the same superiority of numbers there. In three or four days he could have disposed of both the Austrian centre and left. Meanwhile, Quasdanovich would have marched to Mantua, or would have attempted to force the crossings of the Mincio in Serrurier's front. In either case Bonaparte would have had Sauret's, Masséna's, Augereau's, and Serrurier's divisions (probably thirty-five thousand after deducting the cavalry sent in pursuit of the Austrian left and centre) with which to attack Quasdanovich. This plan offered to Bonaparte greater advantages than any of the others. In this way, and in this way alone, could he fight each Austrian column separately, and prevent the junction of the other two columns while he was engaged with the third.

Fourth: By concentrating against the Austrian right, he allowed the Austrian centre and left to unite; and, as we have seen, had Wurmser taken advantage of the opportunity offered he could have united his forces to those of Quasdanovich before Lonato. Why then did Bonaparte choose to concentrate and attack here instead of at Rivoli, where the advantages for securing victory would have been so much greater? The answer is, that he looked not so much to the advantages for securing victory as to the results of defeat. Other things being equal, he would naturally wish to attack first the army that was most endangering his communications.

But the principal reason for this choice of attack was his anxiety to preserve his line of retreat on Milan in case he were defeated. Had he attacked at Rivoli and been defeated, nothing could have saved him; for he would then have had a victorious army in his front and twenty-five thousand on his rear. On the other hand, had he been defeated by Quasdanovich, he could have fallen back on Milan. The results of defeat were more important to him than the advantages for securing victory. Notwithstanding the fact that he seemed always to take great chances in his military career, seemed often to stake everything on the fate of a single battle, seemed almost to burn his bridges behind him so certain was he of success in action, yet a careful analysis of his campaigns shows that no great military commander has ever looked with more anxiety to his lines of retreat than this great master of the art of war.

At Marengo, where he seemed to stake his fate upon a single battle, and where defeat apparently meant ruin, he had carefully arranged a line of retreat by the St. Gothard. At Austerlitz, where he allowed the enemy to envelop his right and cut off his retreat on Vienna, and where he was so certain of success that he issued a proclamation in advance explaining the manoeuvre by which victory would be obtained, yet even here he had provided for a retreat into Bohemia in case of defeat.

The Austrians are a brave people; they fought well in this campaign, but courage availed them nothing; they had a superiority of numbers, but numbers availed them nothing; they tried a new commander, confided in the genius of one of their oldest and most trusted soldiers, but his genius availed them nothing. Everywhere they were defeated and routed; were for the second time driven out of Italy; were in six days hurled back to the mountains from which they had issued. And by whom? By a boy of twenty-six; by one who seemed to violate all their known rules of War, and yet, in spite of this, met with success in every movement. Such genius must have seemed strange to them. It must have seemed strange to their old white-haired marshal, who had won his spurs in many a hard-fought and victorious campaign. It *was* strange; it seems strange to us, even when we know that this boy of twenty-six was one of the greatest masters of the art of war that the world has ever known. It will seem stranger still, when we learn how he hurled back, routed, and destroyed, in the next few months, three more large Austrian armies.

Chapter 4

Bassano and San Georgio

Again the Austrians were re-enforced. Again they attempted to relieve Mantua and to drive the French from Italy. With that fatal persistency in error that Wurmser had exhibited in the previous campaign, he divided his forces; leaving Davidovich with twenty thousand men separated into several detachments in the Tyrol, while with the remainder of his army, twenty-six thousand strong, he was preparing to descend the valley of the Brenta.

The two roads that led from the Tyrol, one to Rivoli by the right bank of the Adige, and the Other to Verona by its left bank, we have already described. From Trent a third road led into the valley of the Brenta, thence followed the river's course as far as Bassano, and then, leaving the river, passed through Vicenza into the valley of the Adige at Verona.

On this last road Wurmser was advancing with his army. His plan was to cross the Adige if possible between Verona and Legnago, and relieve Mantua; or in case the French advanced into the Tyrol, to fall upon their rear, cut off their retreat, and, while Davidovich was attacking them in front, to pen them up in the narrow gorges of the Adige and compel their surrender.

Having received a re-enforcement of several thousand, Bonaparte had altogether about forty-two thousand soldiers. He thought himself strong enough to make an offensive movement. His plan was to penetrate the Tyrol, drive back the Austrians, and effect a junction with the Army of the Rhine, which was then engaged in fighting another Austrian army along the upper course of the Danube. He left three thousand soldiers in Verona, where the fortifications would enable them to hold out for at least two days against greatly superior numbers. He left eight thousand before Mantua. He directed Vaubois, who was at Salo with his division, to march by Riva upon Roveredo; and, with Masséna's and Augereau's divisions, he himself ascended the Adige. Early in September he united these three divisions, numbering about thirty thousand, near Roveredo, attacked Davidovich, defeated him at Roveredo and at Caliano, drove him into the Tyrol, and gained possession of Trent.

Trent was an important point, in that it opened to the French the valley of the Brenta and allowed them to debouch directly upon Wurmser's rear. Until Bonaparte reached this point, he was not aware of Wurmser's departure down the Brenta. He therefore unexpectedly found himself in a favourable position. The Austrian right wing had been overthrown, the left isolated and turned, and he was on its line of retreat With thirty thousand soldiers he was directly between Davidovich and Wurmser, and the former had already been defeated. It was a splendid opportunity for a soldier of Bonaparte's genius. He at once renounced his original plan of uniting with the Army of the Rhine, and decided to march rapidly down the Brenta, in order to overtake and crush Wurmser before he should reach Mantua.

Accordingly, Bonaparte left Vaubois in the Tyrol to hold back Davidovich, while with Masséna's and Augereau's divisions he hurried forward to overtake the Austrians. Marching fifty miles in two. days, he came up with them at Bassano. At Bonaparte's appearance, Wurmser knew not which way to turn. He had expected to find the French in his front; he found them in his rear. He had expected to destroy their communications; he found himself trembling for the safety of his own. He was in a critical situation. Furthermore, one of his divisions had been directed upon Verona a day or so before, and could not be recalled in time to take part in a battle. This gave to the French a numerical superiority and greatly increased Bonaparte's chances of victory.

Wurmser, however, could not escape; he had either to surrender or fight, and like a brave man he decided to accept battle. He was defeated. Quasdanovich's division was nearly cut to pieces, and several thousand Austrians were captured. By this battle, known as Bassano, the Austrian forces were separated: Quasdanovich with the remnants of his division retired into the mountainous district of Friuli, while Wurmser himself with the remainder of his army, numbering about twelve thousand, marched for Mantua by way of Legnago. At Legnago he rested his troops one day, and left a garrison of two thousand soldiers to hold the place.

These twelve thousand Bonaparte tried hard to capture. He ordered Masséna to cross the Adige at Ronco, and Augereau to march by way of Padua and Legnago. At the same time he sent orders to Sahuguet, who was commanding Serrurier's division, to destroy all the bridges and prevent the Austrians from reaching Mantua. Bonaparte's measures seemed to be well taken. Wurmser's delay of one day at Legnago should have been fatal to him. But Masséna, on account of having no pontoon train, was delayed in crossing the Adige; and Sahuguet, who had failed to destroy all the bridges, allowed Wurmser with ten thousand Austrians to slip through into Mantua.

Meanwhile, Masséna and Augereau had closed in on Legnago, and captured the garrison of two thousand Austrians left at that place. This having been accomplished, Bonaparte united his three divisions and advanced to meet Wurmser, who, having united his forces to the garrison at Mantua, had marched out of the works to San Georgio to meet Bonaparte. Bonaparte attacked Wurmser, defeated him in the battle of San Georgio, and drove him within the walls of Mantua.

The advance movements on both sides had begun simultaneously early in September. On the 13th, the commander-in-chief of the Austrian forces, with nearly one fourth of his army, was shut up in the fortress of Mantua. In less than two weeks *the third Austrian army was defeated*. It had lost in killed, wounded, and prisoners more than fifteen thousand soldiers; the French, about eight thousand. At the beginning of this part of the campaign, Wurmser, with his army of forty-six thousand men, had hoped to drive the French from Italy, and to raise the siege of Mantua. At the end, his army was scattered, routed, almost annihilated. Part was in the Tyrol, part in Friuli; ten thousand were shut up in Mantua, and fifteen thousand had been killed, wounded, or captured.

COMMENTS

At the outset, the situation was as follows. The Austrians had forty-six thousand soldiers in the Tyrol and ten thousand in Mantua. Wurmser was free to move with these forty-six thousand against the French upon any of the roads leading from the Tyrol to the Po.

The French had forty-two thousand, composed of four divisions: one before Mantua, two at Rivoli and Verona, and one at Salo. One of these divisions it was necessary to keep before Mantua, in order to maintain the siege there. Bonaparte, therefore, had but three divisions with which to manoeuvre and fight. And, even with these three divisions, he was not free to move against the Austrians in every direction; for he had to manoeuvre in such a way as always to protect the division at Mantua, and prevent it from being isolated and overwhelmed by superior numbers.

The fact that Bonaparte was tied to Mantua, while Wurmser was free to move upon any point, and the additional fact that Bonaparte had but thirty-four thousand soldiers with whom to engage forty-six thousand, gave to Wurmser a great advantage. These numbers are given on the supposition that the forces about Mantua neutralized each other. If we take them into consideration, we have forty-two thousand French opposed to fifty-six thousand Austrians. In other words, a ratio of 3 to 4 in favour of the latter; but in the Lonato-Castiglione part of the campaign the ratio had been 5 to 8 in favour of the Austrians. The inequality in this part of the campaign was so much less that Bonaparte felt strong enough to take the offensive. He believed in the offensive. To win victories, as he had thus far always done, by bringing a superior force upon the battlefield, the offensive is more favourable than the defensive.

On the offensive, a general can follow his own plan; on the defensive, he must conform to that of his adversary. On the offensive, the parts of an army can be concentrated, and the enemy may be surprised and defeated before he can unite the necessary force to repel an attack; on the defensive, the parts of an army must be kept separate, in order to guard all the threatened points till the enemy's point of attack is developed. The Austrian commander also believed in the offensive, but there was one great difference between Bonaparte and Wurmser. Bonaparte believed in it as a means to an end, as a means of uniting his scattered army; but Wurmser left this point entirely out of the problem. Bonaparte united his forces as he advanced to attack; Wurmser separated his forces the moment he commenced an offensive movement. Bonaparte, with his forces at the base of a triangle, moved towards the apex and there won his victory; Wurmser at the apex, moved towards the base and there met defeat.

Bonaparte, beginning active operations with divided forces, united them, and step by step gained more and more momentum, till at last he overcame all opposition and was victorious everywhere; Wurmser, beginning active operations with united forces, separated them, and step by step became weaker and weaker, till at last he found himself a prisoner, his army defeated, scattered, and routed. Though at the outset the advantages were greatly in Wurmser's favour, yet this part of the campaign, from the beginning to the end, was one continual triumph for Bonaparte. He united his three divisions at the head of Lake Garda, outnumbered Davidovich and defeated him at Roveredo and at Caliano; then like a thunderbolt fell upon Wurmser's rear at Bassano, outnumbered him, broke his army in two, and hurled a part of it back into the mountains of Friuli; then again, without a pause, he rushed upon the remnant of the Austrian army, pursued it, concentrated, and outnumbered his adversary for the fourth time, defeated him at San Georgio, and drove him within the Walls of Mantua.

If we glance at the positions of the opposing forces in this and the preceding part of the campaign, we shall find that the French were scattered before the commencement of active operations and united at the close; that the Austrians were united before the commencement and scattered at the close. At the end of each victorious campaign, Bonaparte scattered his forces to collect his supplies, hold his line, protect his communications, and intimidate his adversary. *Genius in the art of war consists in knowing when to scatter your forces and when to unite them.* This maxim Napoleon carried to a perfection never equalled.

It had been necessary for Bonaparte to station Vaubois's division at Salo, in order to prevent the Austrians from advancing upon the French communications by the road on the west side of Lake Garda. Though the lake intervened between this division and the other two at Rivoli and Verona, yet in twenty-four hours Vaubois could have joined Bonaparte at Rivoli by the road around the south end of the lake. Though Bonaparte had but these three divisions with which to manoeuvre and fight, and though at the outset he was necessarily weakened by the separation of Vaubois's division from the other two, nevertheless he was determined to take the offensive.

At the earliest opportunity, he desired to unite all three divisions at Roveredo. In only two ways could this be done: Vaubois could either march around the south end of the lake by way of Peschiera, or march around the north end by way of Riva. Had the first plan been adopted, the French communications in the vicinity of Brescia would have been left unguarded. Furthermore, the distance to Roveredo by this route was nearly three times as far as the other. Bonaparte, therefore, ordered Vaubois to march directly upon Roveredo by way of Riva. Though this plan of concentration, on the whole, perhaps involved less risk to Bonaparte than the other, yet the chances of victory offered to Wurmser at this time are worthy of notice.

He was in the Tyrol with forty-six thousand soldiers. Had he proceeded to the upper end of Lake Garda, there detached a containing force of ten thousand to hold Vaubois in check, and then fallen with the remainder of his army upon Masséna and Augereau, the chances of victory would have been greatly in his favour. He would have had not only superior numbers, but also the advantage of position. In this way, he would have separated Bonaparte's forces, and would have placed his own army in a central position, from which he could have acted advantageously against the French upon either side of the lake. By such a manoeuvre he would have played the same game against the French that Bonaparte, in the previous part of the campaign, had played against the Austrians, Here was offered to Wurmser a great opportunity: the opportunity of attacking with superior numbers an army which was separated into two parts by an impassable obstacle.

Had Wurmser even kept his army united till after the concentration of the French at Roveredo, he would have had forty-six thousand Austrians with whom to oppose thirty thousand French. The chances of victory would still have been greatly in his favour. But at the very outset he began to separate his forces. He repeated the errors that had before caused his own defeat, and also that of his predecessor. Experience taught him nothing. Brave, fearless, and stubborn, he continued to blunder on, neither able to see his own past errors, nor able to comprehend the strategical combinations of his brilliant adversary.

After Bonaparte had defeated the Austrian right and gained Trent, he was between the two Austrian armies with his three divisions. To march against the Austrian left with all this force would have been a hazardous move; for the Austrian right could then have taken Trent and cut off his retreat, which would have enclosed him between the two Austrian armies, where, if defeated, his army would have been captured or annihilated. Bonaparte, therefore, left one division in the Tyrol to hold the Austrians there in check, and to protect his line of retreat; and with the other two divisions he marched against Wurmser.

This movement, too, was in one sense a hazardous one; for Bonaparte knew that he might meet superior numbers. He had but twenty thousand; Wurmser, twenty-six thousand. To overcome this advantage, Bonaparte trusted to his own skill on the battlefield, and to the feeling of his soldiers that they had been victorious so often that they could not be defeated. If, however, he should be defeated, he could fall back, unite with Vaubois, and still present a formidable front. Fortunately for him, when he struck the Austrians at Bassano, one division of

Wurmser's army had been detached Against Verona; and though it was recalled, it did not return in time to participate in the battle.

It might seem that, while the French were in the valley of the Brenta directly on Wurmser's communications, he could have neutralized this advantage by rapidly marching to Rivoli, where he would have been directly on Bonaparte's communications; but Verona barred the way. This place was occupied by three thousand soldiers, who could easily have held out against superior numbers for two or three days; that is, until Bonaparte would have been upon Wurmser's rear. But even if Verona had not been occupied by the French, Wurmser would not, in all probability, have attempted this movement upon the French communications. In accordance with a maxim of war which has been proved by experience, he would have abandoned any intended attack upon his adversary's communications, in order to fight for the recovery of his own. This maxim is stated by Hamley as follows:

> When two armies are manoeuvring against each other's communications, that army whose communications are most easily threatened will abandon the initiative and conform to the movements of its adversary." And he adds further these words: "The importance of this fact [meaning the maxim just quoted] is immense; for the commander who finds himself on his enemy's rear, while his own is still beyond his adversary's reach, may cast aside all anxiety for his own commiunications, and call up every detachment to the decisive point, certain that the enemy will abandon his own designs in order, if possible, to retrieve his position.

Wurmser's delay of one day at Legnago should have been fatal to him, and it would have been if Masséna had not been delayed in crossing the Adige at Ronco. Here, as at Placentia, Bonaparte's want of a pontoon train saved an Austrian army.

Thus far in his military career, Bonaparte was remarkably successful. Part of this success was due to his own genius, and part to his adversary's errors. Moreover, circumstances which he could not control seemed to favour him. Well aware that the goddess of fortune smiled on his undertakings, he often spoke of his "lucky star." We see instances of his good fortune in the movements just described. It was fortunate that he was not attacked before he had united his divisions at Roveredo; it was fortunate that he was not attacked by the whole Austrian army after he had united them there; it was still more fortunate that Wurmser's army was divided, and that an Austrian division was absent from the battle of Bassano. Thus far, fortune had favoured him; but in his next struggle it was to be against him. At Arcole we shall see him driven back and almost overwhelmed by numbers; we shall see his soldiers discouraged, and his generals without hope; we shall see the very elements themselves united for his destruction: but amidst the turmoil and the strife we shall see him, by the force of his genius, still unconquerable, still victorious.

CHAPTER 5

Arcole

For the fourth time the Austrian government determined to make an effort for the possession of Italy. The outlook was favourable to the Austrians. Two French armies along the Upper Danube had met with reverses, and had been driven back. Epidemic fevers among the French troops about Mantua were rapidly diminishing their numbers, and Bonaparte, who now greatly felt the need of more soldiers, was asking in vain for re-enforcements.

By the middle of October, the Austrian forces outside of Mantua were increased to fifty thousand men. Davidovich with twenty thousand was in the Tyrol, and Quasdanovich with thirty thousand was in Friuli. General Alvinzi, who had succeeded Wurmser as commander-in-chief, was with Quasdanovich. Wurmser with twenty thousand Austrians was shut up in Mantua.

To oppose these forces, Bonaparte had barely forty thousand men, situated as follows: Kilmaine with eight thousand was besieging Mantua; Masséna with ten thousand was at Bassano; Augereau with nine thousand, at Verona; and Vaubois with ten thousand, on the Lavis, near Trent. The French had also two or three thousand cavalry in reserve.

Alvinzi and Bonaparte had each a plan of campaign. Alvinzi's plan was that Davidovich should attack Vaubois on the Lavis, while Quasdanovich attacked Masséna at or near Bassano. By reason of his superior numbers, Alvinzi calculated that the French would be defeated; and that Davidovich and Quasdanovich could advance, the former down the Adige to Verona, and the latter along the road from Bassano to Verona. From Verona, with his forces united, Alvinzi purposed to advance to the relief of Mantua,

Bonaparte's plan was to repeat from right to left against Alvinzi the same manoeuvre that he had made from left to right against Wurmser in the preceding part of the campaign. In other words, while Vaubois was holding Davidovich in check, Bonaparte intended to attack Alvinzi in force at or near Bassano and defeat him if possible; then to ascend the Brenta and unite with Vaubois for a combined attack against Davidovich.

Early in November Davidovich advanced from his base of operations in the Tyrol to attack Vaubois at Trent, and at the same time Alvinzi advanced from his base of operations in Friuli to attack Masséna at Bassano, Vaubois was driven back towards Corona and Rivoli, and Masséna retreated towards Verona. By reason of these manoeuvres, Alvinzi could now communicate with Davidovich by the valley of the Brenta along the direct road between Bassano and Trent. By means of this road, he could quickly re-enforce Davidovich's army by a detachment from his own. He did not, however, take advantage of this opportunity; but continued to act separately against the French with his two armies.

Bonaparte, having directed Vaubois to prevent the further advance of Davidovich, advanced with Masséna's and Augereau's divisions to meet Alvinzi on the Brenta. He attacked and obtained a partial success, and intended to renew the attack the next day; but, just at this time learning that Vaubois was closely pressed, he renounced his plan and fell back on Verona. Meanwhile, Vaubois, having lost a third of his force in killed, wounded, and prisoners, was driven back to Corona. Bonaparte himself hastened there, and harangued Vaubois's troops for the purpose of stimulating their courage. Then he hurriedly returned to Verona.

Meanwhile, Alvinzi had advanced on the Bassano-Verona road as far as Caldiero, where he had taken up a strong position. Again Bonaparte with Masséna's and Augereau's divisions advanced to attack him. The attack was vigorous; but the enemy's strong position, his superior numbers, the muddy roads, and a severe wind and hail storm in the face of the French soldiers during the attack, were disadvantages that Bonaparte could not overcome. He was repulsed with loss.

He was now in a critical condition. The two Austrian armies were closing in upon him; already their plan of campaign seemed about to be realized, already their cannon could be heard at Verona. It seemed almost impossible to hold Mantua, and at the same time to prevent the junction of the two Austrian armies. If they united, they could relieve Mantua in spite of anything Bonaparte could do. To save his army, retreat seemed almost a necessity. He had been severely repulsed;

his force was too weak; his generals were losing hope; his men were murmuring and complaining; even the elements themselves, which had so often been favourable to his undertakings, now seemed to be united for his destruction.

In this critical condition he wrote to his government as follows:—

All our superior officers, all our best generals, are *hors de combat*. The Army of Italy, reduced to a handful of men, is exhausted. The heroes of Millesimo, of Lodi, of Castiglione, of Bassano, have died for their country, or are in the hospital. Nothing is left to the corps but their reputation and their pride. Joubert, Lannes, Lamare, Victor, Murat, Chariot, Depuis, Rampon, Pigeon, Menard, Chabrand, are wounded. We are abandoned at the extremity of Italy. The brave men who are left me have no prospect but inevitable death, amidst chances so continual and with forces so inferior. Perhaps the hour of the brave Augereau, of the intrepid Masséna, is near at hand. If I had received the 83rd, numbering three thousand five hundred men known to the army, I would have answered for the result. Perhaps in a few days forty thousand may not be enough.

Though he complained thus bitterly to his government, he affected in the presence of his soldiers the utmost assurance. He encouraged them. He told them that one more effort must be made. He told them that they must not, could not, be beaten. "From the smiling, flowery bivouacs of Italy," said he, "you cannot return to the Alpine snows."

Rather than yield an inch he decided to risk everything. He resolved to throw his army on Alvinzi's flank and rear. This was a hazardous move; but it was the only hope left, and if successful it would show that he could conquer with numbers and even fortune against him.

Alvinzi, who was advancing on the road to Verona, had this fortified city in his front. On his right were impassable mountains. On his left was the river Adige, deep and unfordable. Directly to his rear was the defile of Villa Nova, which he had already passed, and which was the only outlet by which he could retire. To his left and rear was the river Alpon, which rises near Villa Nova and flows south into the Adige. On the left bank of the Alpon, about three miles from its mouth, is the village of Arcole, from which this battle takes its name. The ground between the Adige and the Alpon was marshy. Two causeways crossed the marsh: one, leaving the Adige at Ronco, led to Porcil; the other, leaving Ronco, led to the bridge of Arcole.

Before proceeding to execute his plan, Bonaparte ordered Kilmaine to withdraw from Mantua with two thousand soldiers, to take command at Verona, and to hold it to the last. Then, on November the 14th, Bonaparte, with Masséna's and Augereau's divisions and the reserve of cavalry, in all about twenty thousand soldiers, marched out of Verona by its west gate, descended the Adige, and threw a bridge across the river at Ronco opposite the defile of Villa Nova. On the 15th he crossed the river and began the celebrated battle of Arcole. Masséna advanced upon the causeway towards Porcil, and Augereau upon the one towards Arcole.

The attacks were vigorously made and vigorously repulsed. Bonaparte had his eye on Villa Nova. As it was the only outlet for Alvinzi's army he was anxious to gain possession of it. By so doing he would enclose Alvinzi's army, and might be able to destroy it. But before he could gain the defile, it was necessary to carry the bridge at Arcole. He therefore redoubled his efforts; he urged forward his troops again and again,—even placed himself at their head, where he nearly lost his life by being thrown from the causeway into the marsh. But his efforts were ineffectual; his soldiers were repulsed; the Austrians held the bridge. At night he crossed back with his army to the right bank of the Adige.

Meanwhile, Alvinzi, who had already begun to fear that his retreat might be cut off, was withdrawing his army through Villa Nova. Bonaparte saw this movement, he saw the hope of great results slipping from his grasp. Still he was not discouraged; he could still act advantageously upon Alvinzi's flank.

Alvinzi re-enforced his troops at Arcole, and near there, on the left bank of the Alpon, drew up his main army ready for battle. On the 16th Bonaparte again crossed the Adige and attacked Alvinzi along the causeway leading to Arcole. He was again repulsed. At night he again recrossed to the right bank of the river. Here he learned that Vaubois had been driven from Rivoli, but was retiring slowly and in good order. He realized that he must now retreat, or at once force back Alvinzi.

On the 17th he crossed the Adige for the third time, and after vigorous fighting succeeded, with a part of his force, in driving back the Austrians who had advanced beyond Arcole. With the other part, he crossed the Alpon near its mouth and took Arcole in reverse. This was the critical period; the Austrians were taken by surprise, and gave way.

Then Bonaparte debouched upon the open plain with all his force, and drove them back towards Bassano. After having fought for three days more desperately than he had ever fought before, he was again victorious.

Bonaparte had expected to follow Alvinzi; but, learning that Vaubois was hard pressed, he sent the French cavalry to pursue Alvinzi, and with Masséna's and Augereau's divisions hastened through Verona to re-enforce Vaubois. He entered the city by the east gate three days after having left it by the west gate. Masséna and Augereau joined Vaubois, and together they drove Davidovich into the Tyrol.

Meanwhile, Alvinzi, who had found out that he was pursued by cavalry only, was again advancing towards Verona; but learning that Davidovich had been defeated, he faced about his columns and retired behind the Brenta.

Alvinzi was beaten at all points. The fighting on both sides had been desperate, the loss heavy. In prisoners, killed, and wounded the Austrians had lost about thirteen thousand; the French, about the same number.

During the three days of fighting at Arcole, Wurmser remained quiet at Mantua. Alvinzi did not expect to arrive before the place till November 23rd, and had asked Wurmser not to make a sortie till then. Before that time, Kilmaine was again, besieging Mantua; before that time this part of the campaign was ended, *and the fourth Austrian army defeated.*

COMMENTS

At the outset, the Austrians had thirty thousand soldiers in Friuli, twenty thousand in the Tyrol, and twenty thousand shut up in Mantua. If on our map we connect by three straight lines the three Austrian armies, we shall find that Bonaparte had, within the triangle thus formed, all the divisions of his army. Masséna was at Bassano; Augereau, at Verona; Kilmaine, before Mantua; and Vaubois, at Trent. The French, thus centrally situated, could concentrate more rapidly than the Austrians; At the outset, therefore, they had the advantage of interior lines. But during the campaign this advantage did not always remain with the French. In fact, as we proceed, we see that, owing to peculiarities in the topography of the country, the advantage of interior lines changed several times from one side to the other.

Communication between Bassano and Trent by the direct road along the Brenta was of course much more speedy than by the circui-

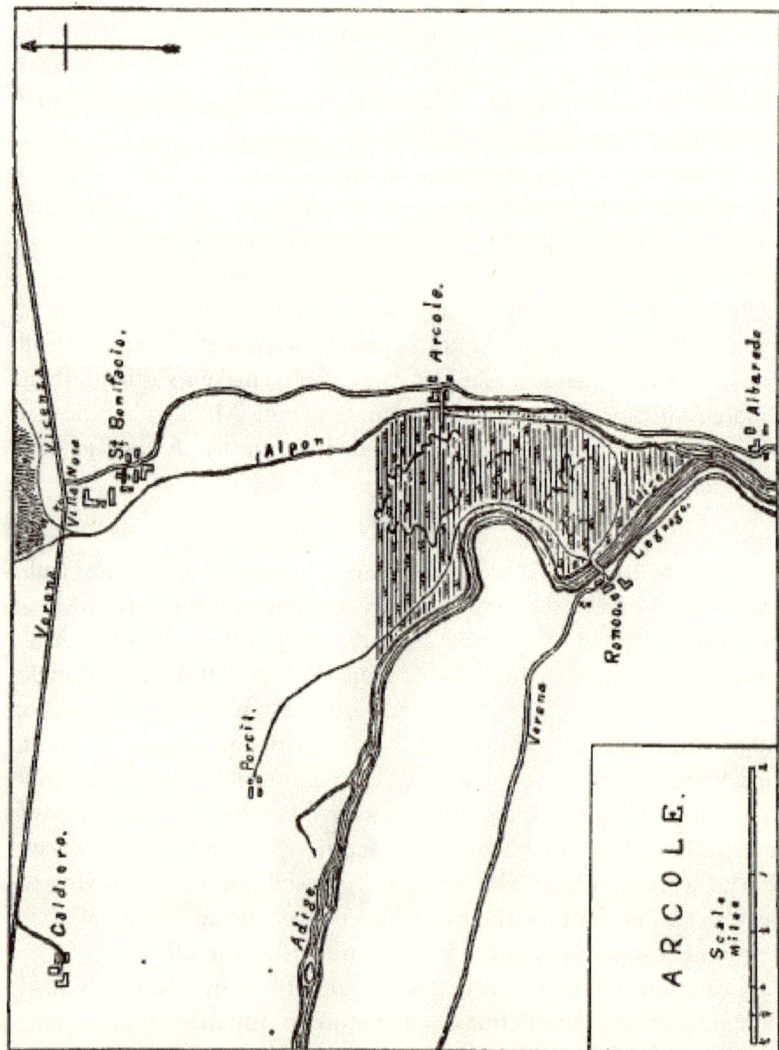

ARCOLE.

Scale
miles

tous route through Verona. The country enclosed by these two roads is mountainous, and impassable for soldiers. As long as the French occupied Bassano and Trent, there could not, therefore, be any direct communication, by either of these roads, between Alvinzi in Friuli and Davidovich in the Tyrol. But, at the start, the French were driven from Bassano and Trent, and these places were occupied by the Austrians. By these simple movements Alvinzi had changed strategically the relative positions of the opposing forces. Occupying Bassano with one army and Trent with the other, he could concentrate by the direct road along the Brenta more quickly than could Bonaparte, who in his operations was restricted to the longer road through Verona. The Austrians now had the advantage of interior lines.

Here was offered to Alvinzi an opportunity which, if he had boldly seized it, would undoubtedly have brought success to his arms. He should have recalled ten thousand soldiers from Trent to Bassano by forced marches, and should have left Davidovich in the Tyrol with the remaining ten thousand to act against Vaubois. Then, with his own army thus increased to forty thousand, he should have marched rapidly against Bonaparte. To oppose these forty thousand, Bonaparte could not have had more than twenty thousand soldiers. By adopting such a plan, Alvinzi would have been almost certain of success. With ten thousand less, he came within a hair's breadth of victory. With ten thousand less, he drove Bonaparte from Bassano, almost crushed him at Caldiero, and amid the marshes of Arcole repulsed him again and again.

But instead of uniting both armies when the opportunity was offered, he continued to act separately against the French along two roads, which were separated by impassable mountains. And Bonaparte at Verona, where these two roads met, had again the advantage of interior lines. From his central position he was enabled to repeat the manoeuvre that had brought him victory at Montenotte and Millesimo, at Lonato and Castiglione; to throw a strong force against Alvinzi, then against Davidovich, and, finally, to defeat both.

In his letter to his government asking for re-enforcements, Bonaparte said:

"If I had received the 83rd, numbering thirty-five hundred men known to the army, I would have answered for the result. Perhaps in a few days forty thousand may not be enough."

These words show clearly what Bonaparte thought. In his mind victory was certain if he could receive this re-enforcement; it was doubtful, if he could not receive it. With such a small addition to his force as this would have been, it seems strange to us that he should have been so confident of success. What disposition could he have made of this re-enforcement that would have changed doubtful success to certain victory? Though this question does not admit a categorical answer, there are nevertheless good reasons for believing that Bonaparte would have used this re-enforcement to strengthen Vaubois.

Vaubois's division, which was attempting to hold Davidovich in cheek, was not strong enough to perform this duty. It fought hard, it lost nearly a third of its strength in killed, wounded, and prisoners; but it was compelled to fall back from position to position. When Bonaparte attacked Alvinzi at Bassano, he expected that Vaubois would be strong enough to hold Davidovich in check. But at the very time that Bonaparte was succeeding against Alvinzi, Vaubois was falling back before Davidovich. Bonaparte, having learned that Davidovich was likely to overthrow Vaubois and raise the siege of Mantua, saw that a complete victory over Alvinzi would under these circumstances have little or no effect upon the result of the campaign. He saw, too, that his own communications were already endangered, and therefore fell back on Verona. The direct cause of his retreat was the weakness of Vaubois. Undoubtedly, then, if Bonaparte had received the re-enforcement that he so urgently asked for, he would have used it to strengthen Vaubois.

Let us suppose that it had been received and so used. This re-enforcement, added to the ten thousand that Vaubois had at Trent, would have increased his force to thirteen thousand five hundred. With this force we believe that, by acting on the defensive, and by taking advantage of the mountainous country, the defiles, and the passes, he could have maintained himself there. Let us suppose that he could have done so, and was doing so, when Bonaparte made his successful attack against Alvinzi at Bassano.

Let us suppose that Bonaparte had attacked the next day, and had been again successful. Alvinzi's army would then have retreated to its base of operations in Friuli. Then, we can imagine Bonaparte giving these orders: "Augereau to watch Alvinzi; Masséna to join Vaubois at Trent by forced marches." Masséna's division of ten thousand and Vaubois's division of thirteen thousand five hundred would have given Bonaparte twenty-three thousand five hundred with which to attack Davidovich's army of twenty thousand. Who can doubt what the result would have been, when we remember that Napoleon never lost a battle in which he was superior to his adversary in numbers?

At Verona, after the Battle of Caldiero, Bonaparte might have taken any one of four courses.

First: He could have remained at Verona.

Had he shut himself up in the fortified town of Verona, he could in all probability have held out as long as his provisions lasted. In this case Alvinzi, who was already at the gates of Verona, would undoubtedly have laid siege to the place. By taking such a course Bonaparte could have prolonged the conflict; but it would have been only a question of time when he would be compelled to surrender. He refused to shut himself up in Verona; and in this connection it is worthy of notice that during all of his military operations he never allowed himself to be besieged in any place.

When the commander of an army is hard pressed, and there is near at hand a strongly fortified place with outlying works of great strength, and provisions and water within, the temptation is great to seek security there. Second rate generals accept such opportunities, but in doing so they make fatal mistakes. The great masters of the art of war manoeuvre for position, and become themselves the besiegers; or decide upon the open battlefield the fate of their fortresses and their armies.

Second: He could have united with Vaubois to attack Davidovich.

Had he united his forces with those of Vaubois, he could easily have defeated Davidovich; but meantime Alvinzi could have crossed the Adige and relieved Mantua, or could have fallen on the French communications with Milan. In either case the difficulties surrounding Bonaparte would have been greatly increased.

Third: He could have retreated with all his forces.

To follow this course would have been to yield up Mantua, to give up the greater part of Italy, and to acknowledge himself beaten.

Fourth: The course he chose, namely, to attack Alvinzi in flank, was the only course left in which there was any hope of success. When he threw his army upon Alvinzi's flank and rear, he hoped to gain possession of the defile of Villa Nova before Alvinzi should withdraw his army through it towards Bassano. Had Bonaparte succeeded in doing this, he would have been directly on Alvinzi's communications, and would have held the only outlet for his army.

Once in possession of this outlet, he expected to annihilate or capture Alvinzi's army. But, in order to gain such complete success as here set forth, three conditions must be fulfilled.

First, that during the flank movement Kilmaine should hold Verona. Otherwise, Alvinzi could unite with Davidovich, which was the very thing that Bonaparte was fighting to prevent.

Second, that, until Bonaparte had destroyed Alvinzi, Vaubois should hold Davidovich in check. Bonaparte's anxiety on this point led him, after each day's unsuccessful attack at Arcole, to cross the Adige to the right bank. He wished to be where he could, if necessary, march to Vaubois's assistance; and he was unwilling to be enclosed in the marshes about Arcole, which might happen if Vaubois should be driven back and Davidovich should gain possession of the crossing at Ronco.

Third, that Bonaparte should reach Villa Nova in time to cut off Alvinzi's retreat.

The conditions were not all fulfilled. The three days' fighting at Arcole allowed Alvinzi to withdraw his army through Villa Nova. In this way he preserved his communications, and saved his army from capture or annihilation; but he could not save it from defeat; nor could he stay the progress of that genius who, though having inferior numbers, brought to his aid the mountains and the marshes, the defiles and the causeways, and with these as re-enforcements marched on to victory.

The Battle of Arcole as planned shows in a remarkable way what extraordinary confidence Bonaparte had in his own military abilities. While his generals were ready to give up Italy, while his soldiers were murmuring and complaining, he was unyielding, courageous, and decided. While everything around him seemed to portend his destruction, he, with an extraordinary assurance of victory, was planning Alvinzi's defeat; nay, more, was planning the capture or annihilation of his army.

Hitherto in this campaign, Bonaparte, though inferior to his adversary in numbers, had nevertheless succeeded in bringing superior numbers upon every battlefield. At Montenotte, Millesimo, the two Degos, Mondovi, the second Castiglione, Roveredo, Caliano, the first Bassano, and San Georgio, he outnumbered his adversary. At Lodi, though he may not have attacked with a force superior to that of the Austrians, he had practically the whole of his army close by and ready for action at a moment's notice. At Lonato and the first Castiglione, which were fought on the same day, though at times the Austrians outnumbered the French, yet he had superior numbers near at hand with which by rapid manoeuvring he won these battles. But in the part of the campaign now under consideration, the odds between the opposing forces were much greater than before.

Here, for the first time, Bonaparte was outnumbered upon every battlefield. No combination was possible by which he could bring a superior, or even an equal, force against Alvinzi. He asked for reenforcements, but received none. He left only eight thousand soldiers before Mantua. He gave to Vaubois only ten thousand with which to hold back twenty thousand in the Tyrol. Even then, he had only twenty thousand with which to oppose the thirty thousand on the Brenta. Such odds were too great. He fell back from Bassano; was driven from Caldiero. Though almost surrounded, almost crushed by numbers, still he did not despair. In the midst of surroundings so dark and gloomy, he saw one chance for success. His mind grasped every detail of the situation. He saw how the marshes, the defiles, and the causeways could be turned to his advantage. He withdrew two thousand soldiers from Mantua, and in this way strengthened his small force as much as he could.

Then he marched down the Adige; plunged into a swamp, and fought along the causeways, where victory depended upon the bravery of the heads of his columns, and where the superiority of his adversary was almost totally annulled. After three days of desperate fighting, the French eagles were victorious. The Battle of Arcole was won. In no other battle has Bonaparte shown himself a greater master of the art of war. In no other battle has he fought more desperately, or shown greater personal courage. In no other battle, among all his splendid victories, has he added greater lustre to his name.

CHAPTER 6

Rivoli

Four Austrian armies had been defeated and hurled back into the mountains of Friuli and the Tyrol; still, the Austrians persevered and hoped for success. Mantua still held out; and twenty thousand starving Austrians there hoped for a victory that would open the gates and allow them to march forth.

By the 1st of January, 1797, Alvinzi's forces in Friuli and the Tyrol were increased to forty-five thousand soldiers; and he determined to make another effort for the relief of Mantua and the possession of Italy. His forces consisted of two corps: the first, seventeen thousand strong, commanded by Provera, was in Friuli; the second, twenty-eight thousand strong, commanded by Alvinzi in person, was in the Tyrol.

In the previous part of the campaign Alvinzi had, from his base in Friuli, made his principal attack upon the French in the vicinity of Verona; this time he purposed to try a new plan. It was to advance with his main force, the second corps, from his base in the Tyrol down the Adige upon Rivoli, while Provera with the first corps advanced from his base in Friuli upon Verona and Legnago. Both corps were to be entirely independent, and each was to strive, by defeating the French in its front, to reach Mantua. By this plan Alvinzi calculated that, while the first corps was attacking the French on the line of the Adige from Verona to Legnago, the second corps would defeat Bonaparte near Rivoli, cut off his communications, and open the gates of Mantua. Accordingly, on the 10th of January, Alvinzi began to descend the Adige with twenty-eight thousand men; while Provera, having divided his corps of seventeen thousand men into two parts, marched upon Verona and Legnago.

Bonaparte had forty-four thousand soldiers. His divisions occupied the following positions: Serrurier with ten thousand soldiers was besieging Mantua; Augereau with ten thousand was on the Adige from Verona to Legnago; Masséna with ten thousand, at Verona; Joubert with ten thousand, at Corona and Rivoli; and a reserve of four thousand, commanded by General Rey, was at Desenzano.

Bonaparte, informed that the Austrians were about to take the offensive, hastened to Verona. He had at the time no definite plan of operations; but was awaiting developments in order to learn, if possible, at what point Alvinzi would make his main attack.

On January 12th Provera, having approached Verona with one division of his corps, was attacked and repulsed by Masséna's division. Nearly one thousand Austrians were made prisoners. The ease with which the Austrians were repulsed convinced Bonaparte that Alvinzi was not making his main attack from this direction. On the afternoon of the next day, January 13th, Bonaparte learned that Joubert was hard pressed and had been compelled to fall back from Corona upon Rivoli. On the same day Rey sent word from Desenzano that no Austrians had been seen on the west side of Lake Garda, and Augereau sent word from Legnago that there appeared to be only a small force of the enemy in that direction.

These facts convinced Bonaparte that the main Austrian attack would be made down the Adige. He at once made his plans accordingly. He knew the advantages that the plateau of Rivoli possessed for a battlefield, and he determined to hold it with Joubert's division, and concentrate other forces there as soon as possible. He sent orders to Joubert to hold the plateau at all hazards. Having already sent orders to Rey to march to Castel Novo, he now sent him orders not to delay there, but to continue his march upon Rivoli. Bonaparte himself, having left two thousand soldiers of Masséna's division to hold Verona, set out with the remainder of this division for Rivoli. At midnight Bonaparte's orders reached Joubert, then in full retreat. He immediately retraced his steps, and by daybreak of the 14th reoccupied the plateau of Rivoli.

This plateau, which was to be the memorable battlefield of Rivoli, is on the right bank of the Adige between the river and Lake Garda. On the north side of the plateau is Monte Baldo and a chain of mountains and hills, part of the main chain that extends eastward from Lake Garda to the north of and beyond Verona. The Adige cuts through these mountains just before arriving opposite the plateau of Rivoli, flows past the town of Rivoli, and thence past Verona and Legnago towards the sea. The two main roads on which Alvinzi marched lie on opposite sides of the Adige, cramped by the mountains within narrow spaces. Between the river and Monte Baldo several roads and trails, impassable for artillery, lead over the mountains, separated from the main road on the right bank by the heights of San Marco. This road leaves the river at Incanale, just above Rivoli, ascends the series of hills that at this point rise abruptly from the river's bank, and passes on over the plateau of Rivoli towards Verona.

Owing to these facts, and in accordance with his plan of battle, Alvinzi had, before passing the mountains, divided his forces into six parts. By his numerical superiority he had forced Joubert to retire from position to position. He expected, however, to find the French strongly posted at Rivoli, and he intended to give battle there and to defeat them. He gave orders that Vukassovich, with about five thousand men, should descend the Adige along the road on the left bank of the river, and attack any French columns on that side; that Quasdanovich, with nine thousand men and the greater part of the artillery and cavalry, should follow the road along the right bank of the river, ascend the heights to the plateau of Rivoli, and attack the French right; that three other columns, unencumbered with artillery or wagons, should pass over the mountain roads and trails and attack the French front; that a sixth column, four thousand strong, commanded by Lusignan, should march around the western slope of Monte Baldo and attack the French left and rear.

By examining these several positions on the map, we see that Vukassovich and Quasdanovich were separated by the Adige; that the three columns forming the Austrian centre were separated from Quasdanovich's column on their left by the heights of San Marco, and from Lusignan's column on their right by Monte Baldo itself. By these dispositions Alvinzi expected to surround the French, and, by making simultaneous attacks upon their front and both flanks, to overwhelm and crush them.

On January 13th these fractions of Alvinzi's army were marching towards Rivoli. They camped that night within sight of the battlefield. Vukassovich and Quasdanovich camped on the river; the other columns, on the southern slope of the Monte Baldo mountains.

During the night, while the Austrians were sleeping, Joubert was returning to occupy the plateau; Masséna and Rey were hurrying forward; and Bonaparte himself, having pushed ahead of Masséna's column, was riding rapidly towards Rivoli. He arrived there after midnight; he saw the lights from the six Austrian camps; he saw that

Alvinzi had separated his columns by impassable obstacles; and he saw that, if he could collect his own forces and hold the plateau, he could probably prevent the Austrian columns from arriving simultaneously upon the battlefield, and, by so doing, could defeat them in detail. In his front were twenty-eight thousand Austrians. He had only Joubert's division of ten thousand; but Masséna would soon bring eight thousand more upon the battlefield, and perhaps Rey might arrive with his four thousand in time to take part in the struggle. At once Bonaparte began to arrange the troops and artillery for battle.

Early in the morning Joubert advanced. The Austrians in his front having no artillery, he succeeded at first in driving them back; and, by directing a part of his artillery upon Quasdanovich's column, he held it in check. But the Austrians soon rallied; the fighting became desperate. An Austrian column attacked furiously the French left and succeeded in turning it. Bonaparte himself rearranged his shattered left, then hurried to the town of Rivoli to bring up Masséna's division which had just arrived there. These troops were hurried forward, and Masséna hurled them against the Austrian right, drove it back, and succeeded in re-establishing the French left. But the French right was still hotly engaged.

Quasdanovich, after hard fighting, had overcome the resistance in his front and was urging his column up the winding road to the battlefield. Already his advanced troops were deploying on the plateau. Lusignan, too, could be seen in the distance deploying upon Bonaparte's rear. In fact, Bonaparte was surrounded; twenty-eight thousand Austrians were advancing upon him. He had but eighteen thousand soldiers. For a moment success seemed impossible, defeat inevitable; but his clear eye took in the whole field: he saw that none of the Austrian columns had yet united; he saw at a glance where the blow must be struck in order to turn disaster into victory; and, with remarkable coolness, he gathered his troops and prepared to throw them, in succession, against the several Austrian columns.

Joubert, in advancing against the Austrian centre, had passed with his right beyond the ascending road over which Quasdanovich was marching to reach the plateau. Bonaparte ordered Joubert to face about his troops and charge Quasdanovich in flank. The latter was overwhelmed; he retreated in confusion down the hill. Bonaparte then hurled the troops of Masséna's and Joubert's divisions against the Austrian columns in their front, routed them, drove them into the mountains and captured many prisoners. Meanwhile, Lusignan, knowing that Bonaparte was surrounded, and believing that the Austrians were already victorious, was advancing to take part in the capture of the French forces. But Bonaparte, having disposed of the Austrians in his front, faced about a part of his victorious troops and advanced to attack Lusignan. Meanwhile, Rey, who was just arriving from Castel Novo, finding Lusignan in his front, also attacked him from that side. At the very time that Lusignan believed the French to be surrounded, he found himself entrapped. Between the two fires he could not escape. He was compelled to surrender his entire force as prisoners of war.

On all sides the Austrians were defeated. Alvinzi's army was almost destroyed. On January 14th nearly eight thousand Austrians were killed, captured, or wounded; and on the next day Joubert, who was sent in pursuit of Alvinzi's army, captured nearly seven thousand more. Out of twenty-eight thousand Austrians with whom Alvinzi began the battle, he had left, on the night of the 16th, but thirteen thousand two hundred and thirty soldiers. Thus ended the Battle of Rivoli, which by military men is pronounced to be one of Bonaparte's greatest tactical battles.

Even this astonishing success did not satisfy Bonaparte. Though he had just gained the most remarkable tactical victory in his already remarkable career, still nothing escaped him. His eye took in the whole theatre of operations. He was anxious about his right, anxious for Augereau, anxious that Provera should not reach Mantua and attack Serrurier on one side, while Wurmser, issuing from the gates of Mantua, should attack him on the other.

In fact, while these operations were taking place at Rivoli, Provera with eight thousand Austrians, about half of his corps, forced the centre of Augereau's line along the Adige, and crossed the river a few miles above Legnago. Augereau, however, fell upon the rear-guard of this force before it crossed the river, cut it to pieces, and captured two thousand prisoners. Provera with the remainder of his force marched rapidly towards Mantua, and Augereau followed in pursuit. The Battle of Rivoli had scarcely ended when Bonaparte learned that Provera had crossed the Adige. Leaving Joubert and Rey to pursue Alvinzi, Bonaparte started at once with Masséna's division for Mantua. Though this division had been marching and fighting continuously for the last twenty-four hours, still, under Bonaparte's direction, it marched all night on the 14th, and the whole of the next day, and on the morning of the 16th was ready for battle in front of Mantua.

Provera arrived before Mantua on the 15th, and the next morning began to attack Serrurier; while Wurmser, issuing from the gates of Mantua, attacked him from that side. But Bonaparte's divisions were near at hand; while Serrurier was driving Wurmser back, Bonaparte closed in upon Provera. The latter, attacked on one side by Serrurier and on the other by Masséna and Augereau, could not escape, but was compelled to surrender his entire force.

In this battle, known as La Favourita, more than five thousand Austrians surrendered. Nearly fifteen thousand had been killed, wounded, or captured at Rivoli; nearly one thousand had been captured by Masséna near Verona, and two thousand by Augereau near Legnago. In three days Bonaparte had, therefore, captured or destroyed more than half of Alvinzi's army.

Meanwhile, Wurmser at Mantua was in a critical condition. For days the garrison of twenty thousand there had been living on horse flesh. Over seven thousand were sick, many had already died, many more were dying. Even the horses were almost consumed. Wurmser could hold out no longer. The victories of Rivoli and La Favourita had destroyed his last hope. He had long and heroically held Mantua, but was at last by force of necessity compelled to yield. He signed the capitulation of the fortress, and on February 2nd the starving garrison surrendered. Thus ended this part of the campaign, in which Bonaparte with only forty-four thousand soldiers killed, wounded, or captured nearly forty-three thousand Austrians. *The fifth Austrian army was annihilated.* For the first time Mantua was in possession of the French. Bonaparte was at last complete master of Italy.

COMMENTS

"To invade a country," says Napoleon, "with a double line of operations is a faulty combination." Alvinzi, defeated on a double line of operations at Arcole, repeated the same error in this part of the campaign. His own corps, having its base in the Tyrol, marched down the Adige to attack at Rivoli. Provera's corps, having its base in Friuli, marched from Bassano to attack Verona and Legnago. Impassable mountains separated the two corps, so that after the movement began there could be no communication between them. This was Alvinzi's greatest error. It gave to Bonaparte the advantage of interior lines, and allowed him to concentrate his forces in succession against the two Austrian corps.

Alvinzi could, at the start, have easily avoided this error. In fact,

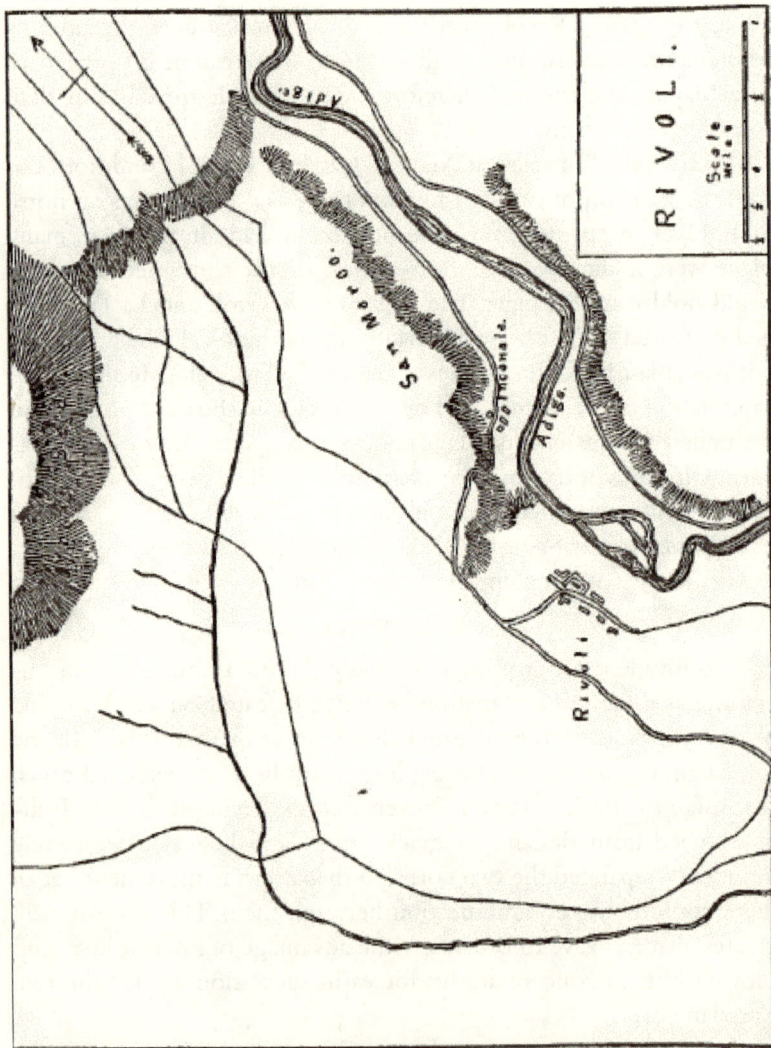

there were two plans, either of which would have been better than the one he adopted. Had he left a small force to act on the defensive against Joubert along the upper Adige, and united the rest of his army at Bassano by the direct road along the upper Brenta, he could then have made an attack on the lower Adige which would have had great chances of success. By so doing he would have adopted a single line of operations, and his forces would have been united into one powerful army, which would have greatly outnumbered the forces that Bonaparte could, by any possibility, have brought against it. Had Alvinzi left ten thousand to act against Joubert, he could then have concentrated thirty-five thousand at Bassano.

As Serrurier's division was absolutely necessary before Mantua, and Joubert's division absolutely necessary at Rivoli, the only troops that Bonaparte could have united to oppose such an army coming from Bassano would have been Augereau's and Masséna's divisions and Rey's force of four thousand. With these forces Bonaparte would have had an army of only twenty-four thousand with which to hold Verona and to oppose Alvinzi's army of thirty-five thousand. The odds against Bonaparte would, in this case, have been greater than they were at Arcole. Such a plan, to say the least, offered Alvinzi great chances of success.

But the other plan which Alvinzi might have adopted offered also great chances of success. He might have left a containing force of ten thousand at Bassano to act against Augereau, and united the remainder of his army for an attack down the Adige upon Rivoli. Such a plan would likely have been successful: for with twenty-eight thousand the result at Rivoli for a time seemed doubtful; perhaps with thirty-five thousand men Alvinzi would have won the battle. Had he adopted this plan, Bonaparte could not have concentrated a greater force at Rivoli than he did actually concentrate there on January 14th; for to withdraw Serrurier from Mantua would have allowed Wurmser to escape, and to withdraw Augereau from the lower Adige would have allowed Serrurier to be crushed between Provera and Wurmser. Further on it will be shown that Alvinzi at Rivoli with twenty-eight thousand soldiers should have been victorious, and would have been, had he not committed error upon error. There is therefore good reason for believing that with thirty-five thousand he would have overwhelmed and crushed Bonaparte.

This plan had one great advantage over the plan previously discussed. An Austrian victory at Rivoli would have left Alvinzi within a short march of the French communications. By marching to the Mincio he could have intercepted the remaining French forces, and by so doing could have ended the campaign. This advantage, however, was more than counterbalanced by the disadvantages which this line of operations offered. The upper Adige flows through a mountainous country, which becomes more mountainous towards Rivoli. In marching down the Adige Alvinzi was compelled to follow the two roads which are separated by the river, and which are confined by the mountains within a narrow valley. In this mountainous country, especially near Rivoli, . there was not room to manoeuvre a large army. In fact, it was with the greatest difficulty that troops could be deployed at all, and then only in such a way that impassable obstacles necessarily intervened between the several organizations.

On the other hand, a small force acting on the defensive could, by taking advantage of the mountains and defiles, hold in check a greatly superior force.

These topographical peculiarities, therefore, made this route difficult for offensive operations, and excellent for defensive ones. From these facts it follows that, though an Austrian victory at Rivoli promised great results, yet so great were the difficulties there that only under the most favourable circumstances could a victory be expected.

But the other route from Bassano towards the lower Adige, lying in an open country where a large army could be easily deployed, is excellent for offensive operations and difficult for defensive ones. Though a victory here would not have allowed Alvinzi to cut Bonaparte's communications, and would not therefore have led to such great results as a victory at Rivoli, yet the advantages here outbalanced all other considerations, and should have led Alvinzi to choose this route for his main attack. He did choose it in the Arcole part of the campaign, and, though he committed many errors, he came within a hair's breadth of victory. In none of these campaigns did the Austrians come so near victory as at Arcole; in none did they experience such a crushing defeat as at Rivoli.

In this connection it is worthy of notice, that, when the commander of an invading army has two lines of operations offered to him, one promising great results under great difficulties and the other offering great promise of an early victory, it is better to select the latter, because a first success encourages the soldier to greater effort. Nothing rouses his enthusiasm like victory. Obstacles, which might at the beginning of a campaign seem insurmountable, appear, after several victories, insignificant to him. His hopes rise, his blood quickens, he feels that he can overcome all difficulties, and, in the future as in the past, march on to victory.

"The defects of Alvinzi's plan," says Derrecagaix in criticising this campaign, "had given to Bonaparte one of his most brilliant triumphs. Again the latter had manoeuvred upon interior lines of operations, while his enemies followed two exterior lines. Nor was this their only mistake. They made their principal attack in a mountainous region abounding in strong positions favourable for defence, while upon the lower Adige they would have deprived the French of this advantage.

"Moreover, the march of Provera's corps could have led to no profitable result. A victory for Alvinzi at Rivoli would have sufficed, indeed, to save Mantua; his defeat, on the contrary, made certain the loss of Provera, without the possibility of bringing any advantage in return.

"The direction which the Austrians should have followed was quite plain. It was that which Prince Eugene adopted against Catinat in 1701, and which Napoleon himself, indeed, afterwards pointed out in referring to the march of Wurmser upon the Brenta. They ought then to have left only a detachment at the entrance to the Tyrol, and have debouched upon the lower Adige with the entire army."

In choosing a double line of operations Alvinzi not only committed the errors which have been pointed out, but in the execution of his plan he continued to multiply mistakes. In his march down the Adige, just before arriving at Rivoli he separated his army into six columns. He intended to have them arrive simultaneously upon the plateau of Rivoli, where he expected to find the French strongly posted. When it is remembered that the Adige separated Vukassovich's column from Quasdanovich's column, that the heights of San Marco separated the latter from the Austrian centre, and that Monte Baldo separated the centre from Lusignan's column, the absurdity of these movements becomes apparent to every soldier.

Under the most favourable circumstances, it is an error to separate an army even into two columns just before a battle; for so many unforeseen conditions arise, or may arise, that it is almost impossible for the columns to attack simultaneously, and only by attacking simultaneously can success be expected from such a plan. Muddy roads, high water, rough country, mountains, defiles, and various other obstacles may delay one column, and by the time it arrives on the battlefield the other column will probably have been defeated. If a commanding general could always foresee all the conditions which would arise, he could so arrange the marches that his columns would arrive simultaneously upon the battlefield; but this being an impossibility, it has come to be a maxim in war that, unless absolutely unavoidable, an army in the face of an enemy should never be separated into parts by impassable obstacles. This, being true of two columns, applies with still greater force to more than two. As the number of columns separated by impassable obstacles increases, the chances for simultaneous attacks decrease in a very rapid ratio.

But this was not Alvinzi's only error. He ordered five thousand soldiers under Vukassovich to march on the east side of the Adige, where they were unable to take part in the battle. In fact, they could not by any possibility reach the battlefield. They were witnesses to Alvinzi's defeat, without being able to raise a helping hand. They pointed their guns in the direction of the battle, and fired a few shots, which had no effect whatever upon the result. They might better have been in the Tyrol, where they would at least have been safe from capture.

Alvinzi made another error in requiring his cavalry and artillery to march with Quasdanovich's column along the river road, where they were enclosed by the mountains on one side and by the river on the other. In this situation, his cavalry could not be deployed, nor his artillery be brought into action. As a result, Alvinzi, who needed cavalry badly, was for the want of it completely ignorant of the whereabouts of the French forces, and the Austrian centre for the want of artillery could make no headway against Joubert's division.

Notwithstanding all these errors, had Alvinzi on the night of January 13th gained possession of the plateau of Rivoli, he would still have had great chances of success. He could easily have done this; for his columns were camped within an hour's march of the plateau which Joubert had already abandoned. Having once gained possession of this plateau, Alvinzi would have been past the critical point in his march; he would have had room to manoeuvre his army; his columns could have united; his artillery could have been distributed to the different organizations, and his cavalry moved to the front and flanks, where it belonged. In fact, he could, by an hour's march, have reached a strong position for battle, where Bonaparte with his inferior numbers would hardly have dared to attack him. That Alvinzi did not seize upon this position was his greatest error. It was the crowning act of that series of errors which together caused his defeat at Rivoli,—one of the most crushing defeats ever experienced by Austrian arms.

It is easy to point out Alvinzi's mistakes after this battle; but owing to the unfavourable situation of his army, and to the obstacles in its immediate front, it is not so easy to set forth in detail the exact manoeuvres which he should have made in his advance down the Adige upon Rivoli. At one day's march from the plateau of Rivoli, where he expected to meet the French in force, his army of twenty-eight thousand was confined within a narrow valley; Monte Baldo and a chain of mountains were in his front, and the only road leading directly to Rivoli was through a long and narrow defile. The problem before him was to reach this plateau and unite his forces there before the French could occupy it; or in case it was already occupied, then so to manoeuvre in his advance as to present a united front to the enemy. His cavalry should have been sent forward in advance of his army, and should have received orders to seize if possible the plateau of Rivoli.

The greater part of the cavalry should have marched by the trails between Monte Baldo and the Adige, while a small column might have marched around the western slope of Monte Baldo, and a still smaller column—a mere scouting party—should have marched by the river road. Following these troops, Alvinzi should have sent a small column of infantry down the Adige, and should have pushed forward his infantry and artillery along the trails and over the hills between Monte Baldo and the river. Having adopted such a plan, his cavalry could have seized the plateau, and the infantry and artillery following could have occupied it; his front would at all times have been protected by cavalry; his right, by Monte Baldo and a column of cavalry; his left, by the Adige and a column of infantry; and, what is still more important, his forces would have been united during the advance.

To this plan it may be objected that the country between Monte Baldo and the Adige was so hilly, and the trails were so few, that this route was impassable for cavalry and artillery. In a measure this is true; still, by dismounting the cavalry and by hauling the guns by hand, the obstacles could easily have been overcome. These obstacles, which seemed impassable to Alvinzi, would not have hindered Bonaparte's advance an hour. To a soldier "impassable" is a relative term; to mediocrity it means much; to a genius it means little. A hill is impassable to an Alvinzi; the Alps themselves are not impassable to a Napoleon.

In this discussion it is a pleasure to turn from the mistakes of Alvinzi to the brilliant operations of Bonaparte.

"It is an easy matter," says Captain Wagner, "to criticise military operations after the event; but it should be borne in mind that the conditions and relative positions of the forces, always set forth with clearness by a good historian, are matters of doubt to the commanders while the operations are in progress."

These words are particularly applicable to the case now before us. When the Austrians began their advance Bonaparte was completely in the dark as to where their main attack would be made. He did not know whether the stronger Austrian column was advancing from the Tyrol upon Rivoli, or from Bassano upon the lower Adige. In fact, he was not certain that an Austrian column was not advancing on the west side of Lake Garda. It was of the utmost importance that he should know at the earliest possible moment where the main Austrian attack would be made, in order that he might concentrate his forces to meet it. Every moment of uncertainty increased Alvinzi's chances of success. Bonaparte realized this, and was therefore in a very anxious state of mind. Couriers were riding rapidly from every part of his scattered army to his headquarters. All kinds of information—rumours, facts, the reports of spies and deserters, the opinions of his marshals and his subordinates—were laid before him. He learned that no Austrians had been seen on the west side of Lake Garda; that Masséna had succeeded in repulsing an Austrian attack from Bassano, and that Joubert had been driven back upon Rivoli. At once he concluded that the main Austrian attack would be made at Rivoli.

When it is remembered that a commander nearly always attempts to deceive his adversary, that the information received at headquarters is often unreliable, that it is frequently made up of rumour, hearsay, and facts, all jumbled together, it is remarkable that Bonaparte should have been so uniformly correct in his deductions and conclusions. Not only at Rivoli, but at Montenotte, Castiglione, and Arcole, his unerring mind deduced from the mass of uncertain information at hand the true movements of his adversary.

In the choice of the plateau of Rivoli for a battlefield, Bonaparte displayed excellent judgement. Though he was in Verona at the time, he had previously passed through Rivoli, and the peculiarities of the surrounding country had photographed themselves indelibly upon his mind. He realized the importance of the position. He could see in the surrounding hills, in the defile, in the river, and in the plateau, the advantages which they offered for tactical manoeuvres. The faculty of seeing and remembering the features of a country through which he passed, and of understanding their value from a military point of view, was one of the distinguishing peculiarities of Napoleon's mind.

At Rivoli, he realized that an hour's delay might lose him the battlefield and the victory. For this reason, every moment of time was utilized in rapidly concentrating his troops. Again, after the battle, he saw the necessity of arriving before Mantua at the earliest possible moment, in order to prevent Serrurier's division from being crushed between Provera and Wurmser. Accordingly, Masséna's division, which had marched all night and fought all day at Rivoli, Was required to march all the next night and all the next day. The minutes and hours which Bonaparte gained in these forced marches, decided the conflict in his favour. Time with him was equivalent to re-enforcements. In every military undertaking, it was an important factor in his calculations.

In these forced marches, the exertion of his soldiers was almost beyond their endurance; but the hope of victory and the presence of Bonaparte himself at their head urged them on. Under his eye they could endure almost any hardship and march almost any distance. The enthusiasm which he could instil into the minds of his men was remarkable. He had that magnetic power which filled his soldiers with enthusiasm and courage, and which in an emergency could call forth all their reserve energy. In this respect he surpassed every one of his subordinate commanders, if not every master of the art of war that the world has ever known.

As we have previously stated, Alvinzi's errors in separating his forces at the outset gave to Bonaparte the advantage of interior lines, by which he could easily keep the Austrian columns separated, and at the same time could combine against each column in succession. In carrying out this plan two of his divisions acted on the defensive, while with the remainder of his army he acted offensively and in force against Alvinzi at Rivoli. It was one of Bonaparte's maxims to take the offensive only on one point at a time. But every exertion was made to collect at this point every spare man. To bring in the shortest possible time upon the vital point—the battlefield—as great a superiority of force as he possibly could, was his great endeavour. He could not by any possibility bring superior numbers upon the battlefield of Rivoli; but by his tactical manoeuvres and combinations he placed his adversary at a disadvantage, and overcame his great superiority in numbers.

His tactical manoeuvres at Rivoli were very similar to his strategical manoeuvres within the theatre of operations. In both cases he brought a stronger force against his adversary at the vital point, while he held back with small forces the enemy's isolated columns.

The strategy and tactics which Bonaparte displayed in these three days' fighting in Italy give us, perhaps, a clearer insight into his system of war than any other single campaign in his remarkable career. His divisions were centrally situated. Strategically, the Austrians almost surrounded him; twenty-eight thousand were marching from the Tyrol upon Rivoli, seventeen thousand from Bassano upon the lower Adige, and twenty thousand were in his rear at Mantua. Having decided that the main Austrian army was approaching Rivoli, he concentrated there his available forces, took the offensive, and, though actually surrounded upon the battlefield, succeeded by his superior tactics in crushing Alvinzi's army; then, before the smoke of battle had died away, he led his weary but heroic troops towards Mantua, where he concentrated once more his forces, took again the offensive, overwhelmed and captured Provera's army, drove Wurmser within the walls of Mantua, and forced him to capitulate.

Such was the end of these remarkable manoeuvres, which for brilliancy and completeness remain unsurpassed by any single military operation in history. Manoeuvres such as these are the foundation of Napoleon's military glory. Not isolated and occasional were they, but repeated again and again in this campaign, till five Austrian armies were successively hurled back before his victorious eagles. Such deeds call forth the admiration of every military student and every soldier. They should encourage us to greater exertion, and to deeper study of our profession, in order that we may gain a better knowledge of those great principles of war which, if correctly applied, would today be as certain in their strategical results as they were at Montenotte, Arcole, and Rivoli a hundred years ago.

CHAPTER 7

The Tagliamento

Before entering upon a detailed description of this part of the campaign, it is necessary to point out the important topographical features of the theatre of operations.

In general terms, the theatre of war embraced Northern Italy and a large part of Austria. The theatre of operations for both armies extended north from the Adriatic to the upper Inn, upper Salza, and upper Mur, and east from Lake Garda to a few miles beyond the eastern slope of the Julian Alps.

Except along the shores of the Adriatic, the country which is comprised within this theatre of operations is very mountainous. These mountains belong to the great chain of the Alps; Over a wide country they spread out in an irregular way into a great number of smaller chains and spurs. Near the water-sheds formed by these mountains several rivers rise; some flow south into the Adriatic, others north and east into the Danube. In the Tyrol these mountains are known as the Tyrolese Alps; farther east, in Northern Friuli, as the Carnic Alps; and still farther east, as the Julian Alps. Between Italy and Austria these three chains form a barrier which is impassable for soldiers except through the passes where the great highways have been constructed.

Within this territory are the rivers Adige, Brenta, Piave, Tagliamento, Isonzo, upper Drave, and their tributaries. The Adige and the Brenta we have already described. The Piave, Tagliamento, and Isonzo rise in the Carnic Alps, and flow south into the Gulf of Venice. Their courses, which are about thirty miles apart, are nearly parallel with one another. The Drave rises in the eastern part of the Tyrol, and flows almost due east along the foot of the northern slope of the Carnic Alps.

From Verona on the lower Adige three roads lead into Austria. The first, on the left, is the great highway of the Tyrol. This road ascends the Adige, passes through Trent and Brixen, crosses the divide at Brenner Pass, descends upon Innspruck, and thence passes into the valley of the Danube. The second, in the centre, passes through Vicenza and Udine, crosses the Carnic Alps at Pontebba, descends upon Villach in the valley of the Drave, and thence passes through Klagenfurt, Judenberg, and Leoben towards Vienna. The third, on the right, passes through Vicenza, Treviso, Goricia, and Adelsberg; thence, turning towards the north, it passes through Laybach and Krainberg to Klagenfurt. Between the last two roads just described an important cross-road passes along the narrow valley of the Isonzo from Goricia through Caporetto to Tarwis. Another important cross-road leaves the highway of the Tyrol at Brixen, passes through Brunecken, crosses the divide near Innichen, descends on Lienz in the valley of the Drave, and thence passes down the valley to Villach.

Such are the general topographical peculiarities of the country in which the French and Austrians were, for the last time in this campaign, to struggle for the mastery.

The fall of Mantua had alarmed Austria. Thus far, Bonaparte had shown himself irresistible in war. Neither numbers, nor obstacles, nor fortune itself, seemed to stop for a moment his progress. He had crossed the Apennines and passed over Italy like a cyclone. Might he not cross the Alps and advance to the very gates of Vienna? Would the Alps be insurmountable to the veterans of Montenotte, Arcole, and Rivoli? These questions Austria was pondering. She realised her danger, and determined to re-enforce her soldiers in Italy, and to send her ablest general to command them.

The Archduke Charles[1] was given command of these forces. He

---

1. The Archduke Charles (Louis de Lorraine) of Austria, son of the Emperor Leopold II, was born at Florence, in 1771. Already at the age of twenty-two he had acquired a high military reputation under the Prince of Coburg, in the campaign of 1793. In 1796 he was made Field-Marshal of the German Empire, and took command of the Austrian army on the Rhine. When he was sent against Napoleon, in 1797, the latter remarked to Maesfield: "Your cabinet has sent against me three armies without generals; now it sends a general without an army." After the campaign of 1799, the Archduke was, by intrigue, removed from the army, and sent into Bohemia in a kind of honourable exile. After the disasters of Hohenlinden and Marengo, he was recalled to favour and placed at the head of the War Department. In 1805 he opposed Massena in Italy, but was absent from Germany at the overthrow of the Austrian monarchy on the field of Austerlitz. In the campaign of 1809, he commanded the Austrian army and was wounded at the battle of Wagram. He was afterward made Governor and (continued next page.)

established his headquarters at Innspruck, and asked that forty thousand soldiers be sent to re-enforce the remnants of Alvinzi's army in Italy. Bonaparte concluded from this that the Archduke intended to assemble his forces in the Tyrol, and from that point make his principal attack against the French. But the Austrian government, failing to see the advantages of this plan, ordered the Archduke to concentrate the greater part of his forces in Friuli, in order to protect the seaport of Trieste and preserve that section of country from invasion.

On February 11th, 1797, there were under arms in the Tyrol ten thousand Austrian soldiers and ten thousand Tyrolese militia, and on the Piave twenty-two thousand Austrian soldiers. On the same date the Archduke Charles arrived on the Piave. The following re-enforcements were to have joined him: twenty-four thousand five hundred soldiers from the Austrian Army of the Rhine, thirteen thousand from the various Austrian provinces, eight thousand exchanged Mantua prisoners, and thirteen thousand five hundred recruits. These re-enforcements, added to the forces already in the Tyrol and on the Piave, would, if we include the ten thousand Tyrolese militia, have increased his army to more than one hundred thousand soldiers.

A few words here in regard to the Archduke Charles will not be out of place. During the time that Bonaparte was contending against Wurmser and Alvinzi in the brilliant engagements already described, the French and Austrians were fighting each other in the vicinity of the upper Danube and the upper Rhine. The French Army of the Rhine, commanded by Moreau, and the French Army of the Sambre and Meuse, commanded by Jourdan, were opposed to the Austrian Army of the Rhine, which was commanded by the Archduke Charles. In this campaign the Archduke Charles had been successful. He had defeated both French armies and had driven them across the Rhine. He had already shown himself to be a great soldier. He was a young man,—younger even than Bonaparte,—and his views upon war were largely the outgrowth of his own successes. He was not wedded to the past. He saw the errors to which in Italy the Austrian commanders had so firmly clung, and he perceived the reasons for many of Bona-

Captain General of Bohemia, and retired to the country. He was the ablest of all the generals that opposed Napoleon. His many virtues and noble character endeared him even to his enemies. Napoleon always spoke of him in terms of high admiration. He ranks high as a military writer. His *Principles of Strategy*, illustrated by the campaigns of 1796 and 1799, were published in Vienna in 1813 and 1819, in seven volumes, with valuable maps and plans.—*Biographie Universelle*.

parte's brilliant triumphs. In short, he was an able soldier, well worthy to try the fortune of war against Bonaparte as an adversary.

Before the capitulation of Wurmser at Mantua, Bonaparte had conceived a plan for future operations against the Austrians. From the Mincio as a base of operations, he purposed to march against the Austrians, to defeat them, cross the Alps, and invade Austria. For the accomplishment of this undertaking, he calculated that he would need a re-enforcement of thirty thousand soldiers. With this re-enforcement and the co-operation of the armies of the Rhine and the Sambre and Meuse, he believed that he could carry the war into the very heart of the Austrian dominions. Accordingly, he wrote to the Directory, explained his plan, and asked for a re-enforcement of thirty thousand soldiers. The Directory ordered Delmas's division from the Army of the Rhine, and Bernadotte's division from the Army of the Sambre and Meuse, to cross the Swiss Alps and join Bonaparte. These two divisions, which numbered a little more than twenty thousand, increased the Army of Italy to seventy thousand soldiers.

Before the commencement of active operations, two facts caused Bonaparte to weigh carefully his chances of success. First: His army was too small for a successful invasion of Austria. The re-enforcements which he received were nearly ten thousand less than the number for which he had asked. Second: The political state of affairs in Italy was unfavourable to the undertaking. The revolutionary governments which he had favoured, the opinions which he had disseminated, and the contributions which he had levied in Italy, had caused much discontent in several of the Italian states. Thus far during the campaign, the discontented states had been compelled to submit to his will; but it was plain that, upon the least reverse to his army, they would not only be willing, but anxious, to take up arms against him. The governments of Turin, Genoa, Naples, Tuscany, Rome, and Venice were all more or less dissatisfied; and the last two, in particular, felt very bitter towards Bonaparte.

In fact, the Papal soldiers had risen against the French, and had planned to attack the rear of the French army. These facts being disclosed to Bonaparte, he at the head of several thousand troops set out, immediately after the fall of Mantua, to march upon Rome in order to chastise the Pope. In the face of the French soldiers the Pope was compelled to yield, but his hatred of Bonaparte and of his opinions remained no less bitter than before.

But the Republic of Venice gave Bonaparte the greatest uneasiness.

He was unable to conclude a treaty of alliance with her. She hated the French. She had sufficient population to maintain a large army, and was already organising and arming her soldiers. Moreover, Bonaparte's line of communication with France, his only line of retreat, passed directly through her territory. Surely, if he should be defeated beyond the Alps, Venice would declare war against him. Nothing could then save him. These facts did not dishearten him, but they caused him to exercise great caution in carrying out his undertaking.

Early in March, while the Alps were still covered with snow, Bonaparte began his advance. The disposition of the Austrian forces at this time was as follows: in the Tyrol behind the Rivers Noss and Lavis there were ten thousand Tyrolese militia, and seventeen thousand Austrian soldiers commanded by Generals Kerpen and Laudon; at Feltre, three thousand commanded by General Lusignan; and on the Piave, twenty-two thousand commanded by the Archduke Charles. It will be seen that the Archduke had altogether in position forty-two thousand Austrian soldiers and ten thousand Tyrolese militia. Inasmuch as the latter, however, were organized for the defence of their firesides, and fought only on their mountains, they should not be considered as forming a permanent part of the Austrian army.

In her instructions to the Archduke Charles, Austria had insisted that he should take position on the Piave with the main portion of his army, so as to cover the seaport of Trieste. This position was faulty, and was difficult to defend. Owing to these instructions, he had not been able to form a plan of campaign in accordance with his own views, but was compelled to carry out, as best he could, the erroneous views of his government. Moreover, Austria was slow in sending forward the promised re-enforcements. Only a few thousand had arrived in the Tyrol; most of the remainder were on their way to join the Archduke; but as they were still north of the Alps, and had to march by way of Klagenfurt, Villach, and Pontebba, it would still take some time for them to arrive.

Upon these facts the Archduke Charles based his plans. He purposed to act on the defensive. His object was to delay matters as long as possible, so as to give time for his re-enforcements to arrive.

On the other hand, Bonaparte, not being able to form an alliance with Venice, determined to leave Generals Victor and Kilmaine in Italy with eighteen thousand soldiers in order to protect his rear, and with the remaining fifty-two thousand to take the offensive against the Austrians before their re-enforcements should arrive. He had the choice of two lines of operations. He could advance either to the north through the Tyrol, or to the east through Friuli. But as both of these lines were occupied by the Austrians, he could not confine himself to either one without exposing his rear to an attack from the enemy occupying the other. He therefore decided that he would send a strong force into the Tyrol to hold the enemy there in check, while with the main portion of his army he would advance by way of Friuli to attack the Austrians on the Piave. His plan was to attack the right of the Archduke, throw his army back towards Laybach or drive it into the sea; then, to march rapidly towards the north, cross the Carnic Alps at Pontebba or Tarwis into the valley of the Drave, unite his divisions there, and march on Vienna.

Accordingly, he sent the divisions of Delmas and Baraguay d'Hilliers to join Joubert's division in the Tyrol, and on the 10th of March took the field in person with the divisions of Masséna, Serrurier, Guyeux, and Bernadotte. The three divisions in the Tyrol numbered eighteen thousand, and the four under Bonaparte's immediate command thirty-four thousand. Bonaparte gave the command in the Tyrol to General Joubert, and ordered him to hold the Austrians in check at all hazards; and, if possible, to drive them beyond the mountains which separate Brixen from Innspruck. He directed Masséna's division, ten thousand strong, to march on Feltre in order to drive back Lusignan; and with the remaining three divisions he advanced towards the Piave.

Upon the arrival of Masséna at Feltre, Lusignan fell back on Longaro, where, on March 13th, Massena attacked and defeated him. In this engagement nearly one thousand Austrians, among whom was General Lusignan, were captured. Having thrown back the remainder of the Austrian division upon Cadora, Masséna then marched towards Spilimbergo, near which place he crossed the Tagliamento on the 16th. After crossing the river he marched by way of Gemona upon Pontebba, so as to threaten the Archduke's right wing and cut off his retreat in this direction.

On the 13th of March, the same day that Masséna defeated Lusignan, Bonaparte crossed the Piave with his three divisions. The Archduke retreated towards the Tagliamento, and Bonaparte followed him by way of Valvasone, where he arrived on the morning of the 16th of March. Opposite this town on the left bank of the Tagliamento, the Austrians were drawn up for battle. The river at this point is fordable. Leaving Serrurier's division in reserve at Valvasone, Bonaparte ordered the divisions of Bernadotte and Guyeux to ford the river and attack the enemy. These two divisions tried to surpass each other in acts of bravery. They forded the river under fire, attacked the Austrians furiously, defeated and routed them, and took five hundred prisoners. This battle, in which Bonaparte and the Archduke Charles met for the first time, is known as the Tagliamento.

Meanwhile the remnants of Lusignan's division, which at this time was commanded by General Ocskay, had succeeded in forcing their way across the mountains to Pontebba; but Masséna, arriving soon afterwards in the gorges of the Alps near that place, attacked and routed them, and drove them back upon Tarwis.

After the battle of the Tagliamento, the Archduke divided his forces. Falling back upon Gradisca with the bulk of his command, he directed Bayalitsch with his division, twenty-five cannon, and a convoy containing a large part of the material for the Austrian army, to march by Cividale and Caporetto upon Tarwis, hoping that he might anticipate Masséna, and, by uniting with Ocskay, be strong enough to hold the passes at Pontebba and Tarwis. The possession of these passes was very important to the Archduke Charles; for the re-enforcements on their way to join him had either to cross the Alps at these points, or to take the circuitous route by way of Krainberg, Laybach, and Adelsberg.

Upon the crossings of the Isonzo the Archduke attempted to make a stand. The town of Gradisca, which was intrenched, covered his left. Against this place Bonaparte directed his principal attack. He ordered Bernadotte to assault the intrenchments, and ordered Serrurier to cross the Isonzo below the town in order to cut off the retreat of the garrison. The movement was successful. The garrison of three thousand surrendered, and the Archduke retreated across the river.

Bonaparte then manoeuvred against the left wing of the Archduke, so as to push him into the valley of the Isonzo. The Archduke, seeing the danger of falling back into the valley, retreated towards Laybach by way of Adelsberg. Bonaparte sent Bernadotte in pursuit. He then directed Guyeux to march by way of Cividale and Caporetto in order to overtake Bayalitsch, and set out himself, at the head of Serrurier's division, to ascend the Isonzo.

Meanwhile Masséna had advanced from Pontebba towards Tarwis, and after a brief action had gained possession of the pass there. The possession of this pass closed the only outlet by which Bayalitsch's division, ascending the narrow valley of the Isonzo, could reach Villach.

The Archduke was in a critical condition; his forces were greatly scattered. The greater part of his own immediate command, pursued by Bernadotte, was retreating upon Laybach; Ocskay was in front of Massena; and Bayalitsch was enclosed in the narrow valley of the Isonzo, where, with Masséna in his front and Bonaparte with the divisions of Guyeux and Serrurier in his rear, he could hardly hope to escape capture.

The Archduke had not yet learned that Masséna held the pass of Tarwis, but he anticipated that such might be the case; for he knew that Ocskay was not sufficiently strong to hold it unless his numbers had already been increased by the re-enforcements that should, by this time, have reached that vicinity. He realized, too, that as the large convoy accompanying Bayalitsch would cause him to march slowly, Masséna would have plenty of time to attack and drive back Ocskay before the arrival of Bayalitsch. On the possession of this pass now depended the safety of a division of the Archduke's army, and that of a large part of his cannon and material of war. He therefore determined to make every effort to hold the pass; or to recapture it, if it was already in Masséna's possession. Accordingly, giving orders for his troops to follow him as rapidly as possible, he hurried forward by way of Laybach and Krainberg to Villach, where his re-enforcements were just beginning to arrive.

Upon his arrival at Villach he hastily collected five or six thousand fresh troops that had just arrived there, united them with Ocskay's division, and attacked Masséna at Tarwis. In this engagement the Archduke was successful; he drove back Masséna and gained possession of the pass. But the latter, realizing the importance of this point, collected his entire division and returned to attack the Archduke. The battle was furiously fought on both sides. It took place on Mount Tarwis, above the clouds and amidst the snow and ice of the Alps. Both sides realized that great results depended upon the success or failure of the battle. Both commanders showed great personal courage, but the Archduke was compelled to yield to his stubborn adversary.

Masséna held the pass. Bayalitsch, attacked in front by Masséna and in rear by Guyeux and Serrurier, was forced to surrender. His division was doomed; about four thousand Austrians were captured, together with twenty-five cannon and an immense amount of baggage and material of war.

Bonaparte had reached the summit of the Alps. The first great step in his undertaking was accomplished. He was on the point of entering Austria. At the start the four divisions under his immediate command had numbered thirty-four thousand. By casualties they had been considerably reduced, so that for this momentous undertaking he had only about thirty thousand soldiers. Such an army was too small. The Austrian re-enforcements were rapidly arriving; in fact, several thousand had already arrived. In a few days he might find himself outnumbered, even overwhelmed, at the very threshold of the Austrian dominions. Bonaparte had foreseen all this before he crossed the Alps. In fact, from the very start, he had calculated that, in case he succeeded in defeating the Archduke, and Joubert succeeded in driving the Austrians from the Tyrol, he would order Joubert to join him in the valley of the Drave.

Accordingly, after the battle of the Tagliamento, when Bonaparte began to see his way clear for the accomplishment of his plans, he sent Joubert orders to march, by way of Brunecken, Lienz, and the valley of the Drave, upon Villach, at which place Bonaparte expected to unite Joubert's divisions with the divisions of Masséna, Guyeux, Serrurier, and Bernadotte.

As the execution of this plan depended as much upon the success of Joubert as upon the success of Bonaparte, we will, for the present, leave the latter in the midst of his victorious troops, while we describe the operations of his lieutenant in the Tyrol.

Joubert ascended the Adige with his three divisions, and, upon crossing the Lavis, found that the Austrians were occupying both sides of the Adige. He pushed forward, attacked them on March 20th at St. Michael, and defeated them. In this battle he killed and captured more than three thousand five hundred of the enemy. The Austrians, followed by Joubert, retreated up the Adige. On March 22nd he attacked them again at Neumark, captured one thousand more prisoners, and forced Generals Laudon and Kerpen to separate their commands. The former fell back to the left on Meran; the latter, to the right towards Brixen. Joubert followed Kerpen, who, being re-enforced by a division from the Rhine, made a stand at Klausen, where Joubert defeated him and forced him still farther back towards Sterzing. At Mittenwald Kerpen was re-enforced by a second division from the Rhine. Again he made a stand; again Joubert defeated him, and drove him across the divide towards Innspruck.

Joubert, having disposed of Kerpen, faced about his columns and marched to Brixen. At this place he learned that Bonaparte had reached the valley of the Drave. Joubert could now fall back and crush Laudon; but as this would take several days, and as it was already the beginning of April, he thought it time to carry out Bonaparte's instructions. He therefore set out to join Bonaparte by way of Brunecken, Lienz, and Villach.

The Tyrol being now evacuated by the French, Kerpen set out to join the Archduke by way of Innspruck, Rattenberg, the valley of the Salza, and Murau; and Laudon, being joined by the Tyrolese militia, descended the Adige, overthrew the few French detachments in his front, and advanced towards Verona in order to join his forces to the Venetian insurgents.

Bonaparte had grave cause for anxiety. After crossing the Alps he learned that the Venetians had risen in arms against the French, and that the two French armies along the Rhine had made no advance into Austrian territory. This news was discouraging. With his communications threatened, Bonaparte could hardly hope to reach Vienna unless supported by the armies along the Rhine. Nevertheless, he determined to put on a bold front. If he could not enter the Austrian capital at the head of his victorious soldiers, he might, perhaps, succeed in making a treaty of peace which would redound to his own and to their glory. With this end in view, on March 31st he wrote a letter to the Archduke Charles, in which he deplored the calamities of war and suggested a treaty of peace. The Archduke replied that he had no authority to make treaties. He did not, however, let the matter drop there, but forwarded Bonaparte's letter to the Emperor at Vienna.

From the summit of the Alps Bonaparte descended into the valley of the Drave. On March 31st he was at Klagenfurt, at which place he wrote the letter to the Archduke Charles. At this time Joubert was about to leave the Tyrol in order to unite his forces with those of Bonaparte; and Bernadotte, who had marched by way of Laybach in pursuit of the Archduke's forces, was approaching Klagenfurt by way of Krainberg.

On the road to Vienna, a few miles north of Klagenfurt, the Archduke had assembled his army. That part of it which had marched by way of Laybach and Krainberg had succeeded in passing Klagenfurt before the arrival of Bonaparte; so that the Archduke had the greater part of his forces well in hand, prepared to dispute the advance of Bonaparte into Austria.

On March 31st Bonaparte set his columns in motion. On the morning of April 1st he attacked the advance-guard of the enemy at St. Veit and overthrew it. On the same day he encountered the enemy in force at Neumark. Here the Archduke had assembled all the remnants of his army, together with four divisions just arrived from the

Rhine. Both sides fought furiously. The Austrians were stubborn, the French impetuous. Finally, after losing about one thousand in killed, wounded, and prisoners the Archduke was compelled to retreat. At Unzmark he again made a stand, but, after losing about one thousand more of his command, was again overthrown. He fell back on the road to Vienna. Bonaparte followed him, and on April 7th entered Leoben.

Meanwhile, at Vienna the Imperial Court was in consternation. The Emperor himself was alarmed. In less than a month Bonaparte had driven the Austrians from Friuli and the Tyrol; had crossed the Alps and invaded Austria; and now, at the head of his victorious army, was rapidly approaching the Austrian capital. The onward rush of these impetuous soldiers was enough to strike terror to the strongest mind and stoutest heart.

The Emperor, realizing the danger, believed the time had come when he should treat for peace. He had already received Bonaparte's letter, which encouraged him to believe that proposals for peace would be favourably received. With this end in view he sent two Austrian officers to Bonaparte's headquarters at Leoben to ask for a suspension of arms for ten days. Bonaparte granted an armistice of five days, at the end of which time Generals Bellegrade and Meerfeld arrived with instructions to sign preliminaries for a definitive peace. On April 18th these preliminaries were signed; the campaign was ended.

During these events Victor and Kilmaine, who were fighting in Italy the Venetian insurgents and Laudon's forces from the Tyrol, had succeeded in preserving Bonaparte's communications. After the armistice of Leoben, Laudon retired into the Tyrol, and the Venetian insurgents were speedily overthrown. Thus ended Bonaparte's first campaign. In less than a month, more than twenty thousand Austrians had been killed, wounded, or captured. *The sixth Austrian army, commanded by the ablest soldier Austria has ever produced, had been beaten in every battle.*

COMMENTS

From a strategical point of view the operations which we have just described are well worthy the study of every military man. The abilities of the opposing commanders, the peculiar topographical features of the country in which the operations were conducted, and the situations of the opposing armies with respect to each other, give to this part of the campaign an unusual interest.

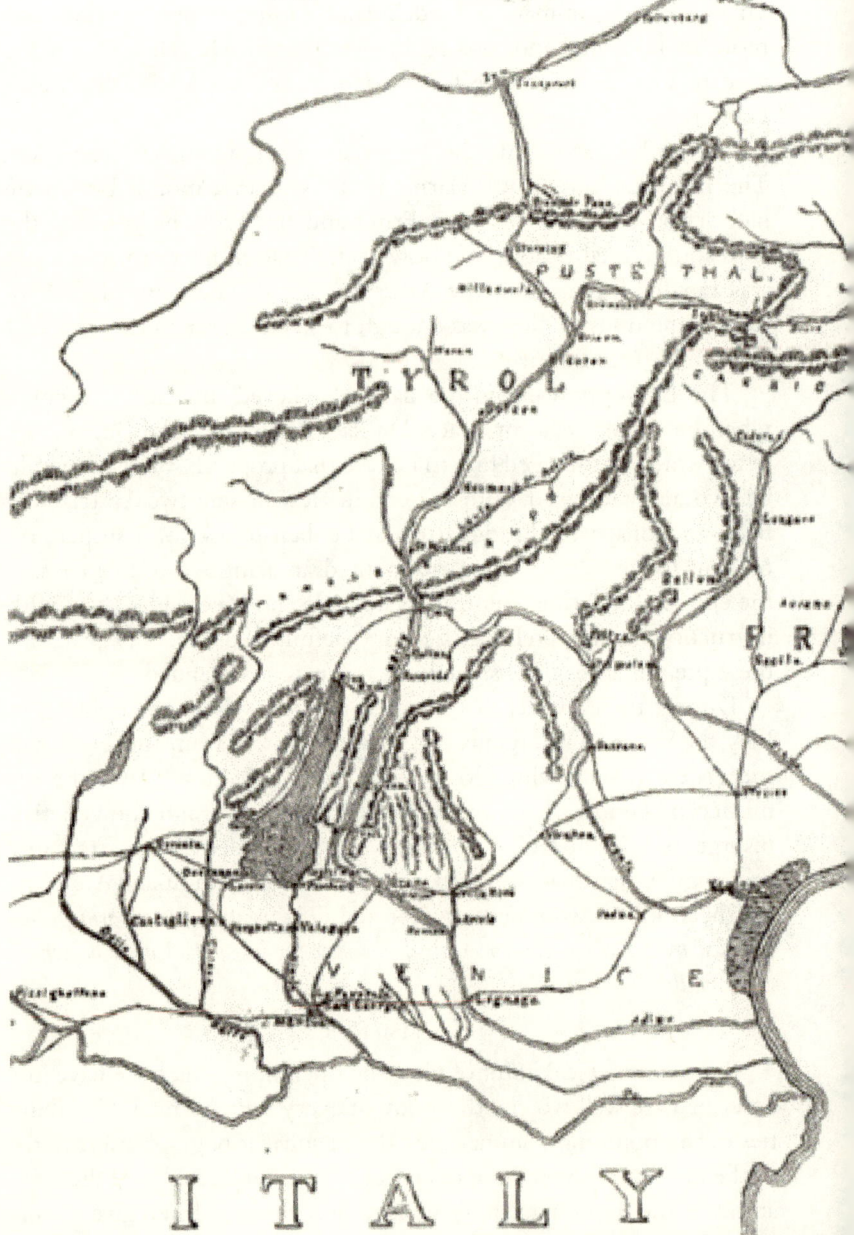

Last part of campaign

At the outset the two principal parts of the Austrian forces were widely separated. The seventeen thousand in the Tyrol were more than fifty miles distant from the twenty-two thousand on the lower Piave, and between the two, at Feltre, was a small Austrian division of three thousand. Along the lower Adige, in the vicinity of Verona and Legnago, Bonaparte had fifty-two thousand to oppose these forces.

The line of communication with Austria for the force in the Tyrol extended towards the north in the direction of Innspruck; that for the force on the Piave extended towards the northeast across the Alps in the direction of Vienna. These, two lines of communication were therefore divergent.

Several rivers and mountain chains separated the Austrians in the Tyrol from those on the Piave. The only communication between them was by the road along the Piave to Feltre,. thence by Primolano and the upper Brenta to Trent on the Adige. But as this road was in front of the Austrian line, it could not be used by the Austrians after Bonaparte began his advance. At the very commencement of active operations, therefore, the two principal Austrian forces became hopelessly separated. Moreover, as they were forced back towards Austria along divergent lines of communication, they became farther and farther separated. In fact, each was a separate army, having its own line of operations and its own line of retreat. From the nature of the country which separated the army in the Tyrol from that on the Piave, and from the plan of campaign which Austria adopted, it is evident that she intended that these two armies should act independently.

Why did Austria separate her forces into two armies? Why did she station one in the Tyrol and the other on the Piave? What are the advantages and disadvantages of such an arrangement? A discussion of the situation should enlighten us on these points.

To prevent Bonaparte from invading her territory was the problem before Austria. Neither of the two Austrian armies was strong enough to take the offensive. Until their numbers should be greatly increased, Austria could not expect to drive Bonaparte from Italy. She might stop his further progress; but she could not expect to do more than this, for aided by superior numbers and the possession of Mantua she had not been able even to hold Italy.

By two routes only could Bonaparte invade Austria. One was by the great highway of the Tyrol to the valley of the upper Danube; the other was by several roads across the Alps to Klagenfurt, thence by the single road to Vienna. By stationing one army in the Tyrol and another on the Piave, so as to cover these two routes, Austria expected to prevent the advance of Bonaparte. There was also an additional reason for this arrangement. The army on the Piave covered the roads which lead directly to Trieste. This place was the only important Austrian seaport. It was a large and flourishing city, surrounded by a fertile country. As a considerable part of the supplies for the Austrian forces came from this city, it was important that it should be protected. Furthermore, an army on the Piave, if defeated, could fall back first on the Tagliamento and then on the Isonzo, and there find good defensive positions.

Did these reasons justify Austria in such an arrangement of her forces? Were the two armies advantageously situated for preventing the invasion of her territory? This arrangement was certainly faulty; in adopting it, Austria committed many errors.

First: Had the two Austrian armies been united, they would have constituted a strong force; separated, they were both weak.

Second: With an Austrian army in the Tyrol and another on the Piave, Bonaparte could with a small force hold one in check, while he brought an overwhelming force against the other.

Third: As soon as active operations began, Bonaparte could re-enforce Joubert in the Tyrol, or Joubert could re-enforce Bonaparte on the Tagliamento, by the road through Feltre and Trent, while neither of the Austrian armies could re-enforce the other by the strength of a single man.

Fourth: As a division of only three thousand soldiers covered the direct road into Austria by way of Pontebba pass, Bonaparte could, by defeating this division, easily gain possession of this important point.

Fifth: It was impossible for the Austrian re-enforcements, coming from the upper Danube, to join the army on the Piave without making a circuitous march by way of Klagenfurt. Had the two armies been united in the Tyrol, these re-enforcements could have arrived there two weeks earlier.

Sixth: Instead of allowing the Archduke Charles to form his own plan of campaign, the Austrian government insisted that he should carry out plans which were faulty, and which he did not approve. He was hampered by the instructions of his government, and committed from the start to a system of errors sufficient to discourage the ablest soldier. He was well worthy the confidence of his government, had already proved this, and should have been allowed to conduct the entire campaign in his own way.

Seventh: To prevent Bonaparte from invading Austria by way of Klagenfurt it was not necessary to station an army directly on this route. The Austrian forces united into one army in the vicinity of Trent would have answered the same purpose; for in that case Bonaparte could not advance eastward beyond the Adige without exposing his flank and rear. Bonaparte would never have attempted to invade Austria by way of Klagenfurt while the entire Austrian army at Trent remained undefeated. Such a manoeuvre would have carried him from, instead of towards, his enemy; would have lengthened and weakened his line of communications; and would have exposed his flank and rear to the enemy's attack. Such a manoeuvre would have been the height of folly, and would in all probability have resulted in the capture or annihilation of the Army of Italy.

The effect produced by stationing an army on the Piave was, then, exactly contrary to what the Austrian government expected. An army there did not prevent invasion, but encouraged it.

For similar reasons it was not necessary, in order to protect Trieste, for the army on the Piave to cover the roads which lead to that city. In fact, an army of forty-two thousand in the Tyrol would have protected Trieste more effectually than the same army could have done had it covered the roads which lead directly to that place. Perhaps this paradoxical statement needs proof. It will be conceded, for the reasons given above, that Bonaparte would not have advanced upon Trieste while an Austrian army of forty-two thousand remained undefeated in the Tyrol. In either case, then, whether the Austrian army were on his flank in the Tyrol, or directly in his front covering Trieste, it would be necessary to defeat it before advancing. But the Tyrol was favourable for defence. For this purpose, the rivers, mountains, and defiles gave to it great strength. Moreover, an army there would directly cover its communications with Austria. If defeated, it could fall back to another good position, fight again, and still present a formidable front. The reverse of this was true for an army covering Trieste. The country was more open and the rivers were fordable. Moreover, as in this position the communications would extend to the right and rear of the Austrian army, Bonaparte could, by defeating the right wing, cut off and seize these communications.

In this connection it is worthy of notice that when a government sends forth an army to protect a capital, a portion of country, a large city, or an important seaport, it is not always necessary that the army should cover the roads which lead directly to the place; in fact, it is often advantageous to take up a flanking position where the communications of the army are protected, and where it can attack the flank of the enemy if he advances. But these questions should be decided by the commander of the army, and not by the government. The best results will invariably be obtained by leaving the diagnosis of disease to doctors, politics to politicians, and military matters to military men.

We have pointed out with considerable detail the errors due to the arrangement of the Austrian forces. Was there no advantage arising from such an arrangement? As the situation of the two Austrian armies compelled Bonaparte to divide his forces, it might seem that this was an advantage to the Austrian side; for in dividing his army he must necessarily have weakened his side. This is true; nevertheless, after the division of his forces, he still had the advantage of interior lines; so that the disadvantage to him arising from a division of his forces was not so great as the disadvantage to the Austrians arising from the same cause.

It is evident from what has already been said that the two Austrian armies should have been united in the Tyrol. The plan of campaign should have been to act on the defensive till the Austrian re-enforcements arrived; then to take the offensive against Bonaparte, either down the Brenta towards Arcole, or along the west side of Lake Garda towards Brescia. Had this plan been adopted, the Austrian re-enforcements could have joined the Archduke two weeks earlier than they did; and while awaiting their arrival, the ten thousand Tyrolese militia would have materially strengthened the Austrian army. By the middle of March the Archduke could have been ready to take the offensive with an army of more than eighty thousand soldiers. To oppose such an army Bonaparte had but seventy thousand. The advantages would have been with the Archduke; and though he would probably have been defeated and driven back into the Tyrol, yet even then he might have saved Austria from invasion.

Starting from the vicinity of Verona and Legnago on the Adige, Bonaparte had the choice of two lines of operations. As previously stated, he could operate towards the north against the Austrians in the Tyrol, or towards the east against the Archduke Charles in Friuli; but if he confined himself entirely to either line, the Austrian army occupying the other could fall upon his rear. He was, therefore, compelled to divide his forces. He decided to send a strong force into the Tyrol to hold the Austrians there in check, while he marched in person with the main part of his army against the Archduke. Three reasons led him to choose the route through Friuli as his principal line of operations.

First: The shores of the Adriatic were better suited for offensive operations; a large army there could be easily manoeuvred. On the other hand, the Tyrol was better suited for defensive operations; a containing force there could operate to advantage.

Second: As the line of communications of the Archduke's army was to the right and rear of his right wing, Bonaparte could, by defeating it, seize the Archduke's line of retreat, and by so doing might be able either to capture his army or drive it into the sea.

Third: This route led directly towards the Austrian capital. To an invading army the possession of the capital of a country is always of the utmost importance; as a rule, when it is taken the war ends.

"A capital city," says Dufour, "is a strategic point of great importance, because it regulates or greatly influences the public opinion of the nation, contains abundant resources of every kind, the loss of which may greatly paralyze the enemy; and to the minds of a large portion of the people all hope of successful defence is lost when an invading army has reached the heart of the state."

Having noticed the reasons why Bonaparte chose this route for his main line of operations, we will now point out some of the distinguishing features of this part of the campaign. For the first time since taking command of the Army of Italy Bonaparte was stronger numerically than his adversary. Omitting for the present the eighteen thousand French soldiers left in Italy to protect the French rear, and also the re-enforcements on their way to join the Austrian armies, there remained at the beginning of active operations fifty-two thousand French soldiers with whom to oppose forty-two thousand Austrians and the Tyrolese militia. Though the militia numbered ten thousand, only a part joined the Austrians at the beginning of active operations. Moreover, the value of the militia as a fighting force, for reasons already given, was considerably less than that of the same number of Austrian soldiers.

At the outset, Bonaparte had, therefore, a numerical superiority of several thousand. To this superiority in numbers is due the absence of those brilliant combinations and manoeuvres which were such distinguishing features in the operations previously described. It will be noticed, however, that, had Bonaparte been hard pressed at this time, his forces were favourably situated for concentrating overwhelm-

90

ing numbers against either Austrian army. On March 13th, the day Masséna attacked Lusignan, the opposing forces were situated as follows: Bonaparte on the Piave had twenty-four thousand soldiers, and the Archduke Charles in his front had twenty-two thousand; Masséna at Longaro had ten thousand to oppose Lusignan's division of three thousand; and Joubert in the Tyrol had eighteen thousand to oppose seventeen thousand Austrians and ten thousand militia.

In this situation Bonaparte's army consisted of two strong wings and a centre. Had Joubert been hard pressed, Masséna could have joined him. This junction would have given Joubert twenty-eight thousand soldiers with whom to oppose seventeen thousand Austrians and ten thousand militia. Had Bonaparte been hard pressed, he could have called Masséna to him; and would then have had thirty- four thousand soldiers with whom to oppose twenty-two thousand Austrians. In fact, though not at all hard pressed, he exercised the caution of having Masséna near him at the battle of the Tagliamento.

It will be noticed that, on the very day of this battle, Masséna crossed the Tagliamento near Spilimbergo only a short distance from the battlefield. Though his objective at that time was the pass at Pontebba, yet he so regulated his marches that, had it been necessary, he could have joined Bonaparte before the battle. In the detailed orders sent on the afternoon of March 13th by Bonaparte to Massena are the following paragraphs bearing upon this point:—

The enemy is retiring, and appears to have decided to take position behind the Tagliamento. The general-in-chief hopes to deliver a blow which shall decide the fate of the campaign, and cover the Army of Italy with new laurels. He is certain that Prince Charles commands. . . .

The general-in-chief orders General Masséna to set out tomorrow for Belluno, and move towards the Tagliamento; he desires him to be at Aviano tomorrow evening, where he will receive new orders. . . .

Although the general-in-chief presumes that the forces which he has at this moment are sufficient to insure victory, he may think it well to delay his attacks for a day in order that the brave Masséna division may participate.

When Bonaparte began his advance against the Archduke, the latter fell back towards Trieste. Undoubtedly, the orders of his government caused him to retreat in this direction. Had he taken a position

91

directly covering the roads to Klagenfurt by way of Pontebba and Tarwis, he would have been better able to prevent the invasion of Austria. His right flank could not then have been so easily turned; and though he must have been defeated, he could have fallen back across the Alps, and could have held the passes at Pontebba and Tarwis with strong detachments long enough to receive the greater part of the Austrian re-enforcements. Had the Archduke united in this way all his available forces near Villach, and held at the same time the passes, Bonaparte would have found great difficulty in forcing his way across the Alps; and even had he succeeded in doing this, the Archduke was still in a position to defeat the heads of the French columns as they debouched from the passes into the valley of the Drave.

It is evident, too, that, if this plan had been adopted, Bonaparte would not have attempted to invade Austria by way of Laybach and Krainberg; for the moment he passed the Isonzo, the Archduke could have descended from Pontebba and Tarwis upon the French rear, and could have cut off their communications without in the least endangering his own.

After the battle of the Tagliamento, the Archduke Charles divided his army. He sent Bayalitsch's division by way of Udine and Caporetto towards Tarwis, while with the remainder of his army he fell back on the Isonzo so as to cover Trieste. When the Archduke detached this division, he expected that it would gain the pass at Tarwis and hold it, thus insuring the retreat of his immediate command by the valley of the Isonzo. Bonaparte saw in this situation a chance to entrap his adversary. He directed Masséna to seize the pass at Tarwis, and then with Serrurier's and Bernadotte's divisions he crossed the Isonzo below the Archduke, and manoeuvred to turn him into the valley of the Isonzo. Had Bonaparte succeeded in doing this, the Archduke could not have escaped. Enclosed within this narrow valley by Masséna's division in his front and by Bernadotte's, Serrurier's, and Guyeux's divisions in his rear, the Archduke would have been compelled to surrender his army. Fortunately for him he saw the danger in time to avoid it by retreating towards Laybach.

It was at this time that he hurried to Villach in order to collect a force to attack the pass at Tarwis. The possession of this pass had become of the greatest importance. In fact, it was the key to the situation. If the pass were held by Masséna, Bonaparte could not only destroy Bayalitsch, but he could also debouch from the pass upon Villach with the divisions of Masséna, Serrurier, and Guyeux, drive back the

Austrian re-enforcements, gain possession of Klagenfurt, and in this way cut off, capture, or destroy the Austrian forces marching by way of Laybach and Krainberg. On the other hand, if the pass were held by the Archduke, he could unite his scattered forces in the vicinity of Tarwis or Villach, and present a formidable front to Bonaparte's advance.

Moreover, Bayalitsch would escape capture, and the immense amount of supplies and material of war with him would be saved to the Austrian army. It is to the credit of the Archduke Charles that he comprehended the situation, and hurried to Tarwis to fight for the possession of this important point. It is to his credit that, under such unfavourable circumstances, he fought so desperately and showed such personal courage. Though he could not save Bayalitsch, nor stop the progress of Bonaparte, he had the satisfaction of knowing that this battle, fought so furiously, delayed his adversary long enough to allow the Austrian divisions coming from Laybach to escape capture or annihilation.

Though at the start Bonaparte had in his mind the plan of drawing Joubert to him by the valley of the Drave, yet this movement depended not only on Bonaparte's success in Friuli, but also on Joubert's success in the Tyrol. Had not Bonaparte crossed the Alps, Joubert would not have entered the valley of the Drave. There was, in fact, but one distinct line of operations; for the force in the Tyrol under Joubert was essentially a containing force. Joubert's object was not to invade Austria, but to protect the rear of the Army of Italy. As Bonaparte advanced farther and farther into Austria, it became of the utmost importance that Joubert should hold in check the Austrians and militia in the Tyrol.

For this purpose Bonaparte had given him eighteen thousand soldiers. There were at this time in the Tyrol seventeen thousand Austrians and ten thousand Tyrolese militia. Though the result showed that Joubert was stronger than his enemy, yet at the beginning of active operations there was nothing to indicate that he would win such success against such odds. In fact, Bonaparte himself was doubtful whether Joubert could hold in check the forces of the enemy in the Tyrol. This fact is clearly shown in the following orders:—

Headquarters, Sacile,
March 15th, 1797.

To General Joubert:—In order to form a junction of the divisions which are in the Tyrol and those in Friuli, it is necessary for the latter to cross the Tagliamento, seize the position at Osoppo, force the passes of Pontebbana (Pontebba), and reach the valley of the Drave.

The Tyrol divisions should arrive at Brixen and drive the enemy beyond the high chain of mountains separating Innspruck from Brixen. But events may occur which the contingencies of war require should be provided for in advance.

First: The Tyrol divisions may be beaten and obliged to fall back upon the Mori line, or even that of Rivoli; be forced into the intrenched camp of Castelnuovo (Castel Novo), and reduced to the defence of the Mincio; or even be compelled to shelter themselves in Mantua.

Second: The enemy may endeavour to penetrate by Feltre and Primolano, in an attempt to break our communications; this, in the present condition of things, appears to me very difficult.

Third: It may happen that, by one movement or another, the divisions which are in Friuli may be outflanked on the right or left, and that a head of column of the enemy may hence gain the Piave, and even the Brenta, before the Friuli divisions.

Should the first hypothesis prove correct, but only in this case, you will make use of the order which I send you, giving you command of the divisions located in the district of Mantua, as well as in Lombardy and the whole of the country comprised between the Oglio and the Adige.

In every case, you must provision and hold Peschiera, Porto-Legnago, Mantua, and Pizzighettone; place yourself between Mantua and the Po, in a position to supply yourself by this river and to fall upon the rear of the enemy if he dare to advance into the Milanese; inform General Sahuguet that he is to concentrate all his forces in the castle of Ferrara. I shall give you, moreover, as the exigencies of events demand, all necessary instructions, not doubting that, under all circumstances, you will act conformably to the spirit of the war which we are now waging.

You understand that it is essential, in case you are beaten, to dispute every position, and to make use of all resources of art, and of all natural features of the ground, in order to give the Friuli divisions time to take proper measures.

You will find enclosed herewith, Citizen General, detailed instructions upon the different cases which may arise.

Prepare to attack Botzen by the most convenient direction, taking the snows into consideration.

Tomorrow we shall make a crossing of the Tagliamento, which it is said the enemy intends disputing. I desire you to begin your movement on the 27th or 28th. If the weather continues as fine as today, and fortune favours us, I calculate upon being in the defiles of Pontebbana (Pontebba) on the 30th; that is, upon the road leading from Udine to Klagenfurt. I shall write from Udine in greater detail.

You will find enclosed instructions for your future government, should you succeed in seizing a part of the Tyrol.

Bonaparte.

Says Derrecagaix:—

In his combination, Bonaparte seemed to adopt two lines of operations: one through Friuli, the other through the Tyrol and the Pusterthal. But this was only in appearance. The line indicated to Joubert was to be followed only in case of the success of the main forces. It extended through a country impracticable for the enemy, and was to be connected by means of Masséna's division with the operating line of the principal army.

We should not, moreover, forget that in moving toward the Noric and Julian Alps, Bonaparte had upon his left a hostile corps, established in the midst of the Tyrol, and ready to cut his communications by the valley of the Adige, aided by the warlike inhabitants of this country. Joubert's corps had then a special mission. It was a necessary detachment, but it was only a detachment. The line of operations was that pursued by the bulk of our forces.

In reality, the decisive movement, that of the army proper, was to take place upon a single line of operations, the line in Friuli.

Though Bonaparte was everywhere successful in his combinations, he has nevertheless been severely criticised for having adopted in this part of the campaign two distinct lines of operations. In his own language he has stated these criticisms and his replies to them as follows:—

Was not the march into Germany by two lines of operations, those of the Tyrol and Pontebba, a violation of the principle that an army should have but one line of operations? Was not the union of these two corps in Carinthia, so distant from the point of departure, contrary to the principle of never joining columns in the face of the enemy? Would it not have been preferable to have left from seven thousand to eight thousand men before Trent upon the defensive, and to have collected ten thousand or twelve thousand more upon the Piave? This plan would have avoided the necessity of carrying on the war in the Tyrol, a difficult theatre; it would not have been exposed to chances unfavourable for a junction of the columns; and at the outset of the campaign all the forces would have been concentrated.

Neither of the principles above cited has been violated. If only eight thousand men had been left with Joubert upon the Avicio (Lavis), he would have been attacked, and the corps of Davidovich (Kerpen's and Laudon's forces) would have reached Verona before the French army arrived at Villach. For the purpose of maintaining himself upon the Avicio, Joubert required at least fourteen thousand men. It seemed preferable to leave his forces undiminished, thus giving him a numerical superiority which would enable him to defeat Davidovich, shatter and demoralize him, and drive him beyond the Brenner. The Tyrol is a difficult region, but it is fatal to the conquered. The French troops had acquired a great superiority over the Germans.

Germany was not entered by two lines of operations, since the Pusterthal is on this side of the crest of the Alps, and as soon as Joubert had passed Lienz, the line of operation was that of Villach and Pontebba. Junction of the two corps was not made in front of the enemy, for when Joubert left Brixen to move to the right upon Spittal by the Pusterthal or the valley of the Drave, the main army had arrived at Klagenfurt, and had patrols as far as Lienz. The Archduke, then, could devise no manoeuvre to prevent this junction. Joubert, up to the time of the battle of the Tagliamento, remained upon the defensive.

After this battle he attacked, beat, and destroyed the greater part of Davidovich's corps, and threw it back beyond the Brenner; all this without risk, since, had he been beaten, he would simply have fallen back from position to position in Italy. When he learned that the army had passed the Julian Alps and the Drave, he made his junction movement by way of the Pusterthal, which was also without inconvenience. This operation, rapidly executed, was indeed conformable to all rules; it should have had, and indeed did have, every kind of advantage.

Everywhere victory had crowned the Army of Italy. Bonaparte had crossed the Alps; Joubert was about to join him. With all his available forces about to unite into one army, Bonaparte was ready to march on the Austrian capital. His generals were confident of further success; his soldiers were filled with enthusiasm. In an army where all had tasted victory, none dreamed of defeat. Bonaparte alone saw the difficulties of the undertaking. He knew that his rear was in danger; he knew that his line of communication was weak, and would become weaker and weaker the farther he advanced towards Vienna; he knew that the armies of the Rhine and the Sambre and Meuse could not co-operate with him in his bold undertaking.

It seemed almost folly to march into the heart of the Austrian dominions, and expect to conquer the Austrian monarchy at the head of only fifty thousand soldiers. Moreover, as he advanced, his army was constantly diminishing in numbers, while the Austrian army was being continually re-enforced. The Hungarians were about to rise and join their forces to those of the Archduke Charles. Volunteers for the defence of the Austrian capital were already organizing. Soon, Bonaparte would find himself in the presence of superior numbers; soon, he might be crushed by overwhelming odds. Against odds sufficiently great, the greatest must eventually fall.

Under these circumstances, Bonaparte offered peace; he agreed to the armistice, and signed the preliminaries for a treaty of peace. His caution decided him in this course. His caution caused him to halt his victorious army almost within sight of the Austrian capital. His caution enabled him to end with brilliancy one of the most wonderful campaigns ever planned and fought.

Had he been as cautious in after years, he might have died Emperor of the French, "in the midst of the French people whom he loved so well."[2] Had he been as cautious in after years, he might never have fallen at Waterloo,—might never have been banished to that lone rock made famous by his great name.

---

2. "It is my wish that my ashes may repose on the banks of the Seine, in the midst of the French people whom I have loved so well."—The will of Napoleon.

CHAPTER 8

General Comments

At the beginning of this campaign the outlook is most unfavourable to Bonaparte. Taking command of the Army of Italy when it is ill fed and ill equipped, when it is deficient in siege artillery, in pontoon equipage, and means of transportation, he surmounts all these difficulties, crosses the Apennines in the face of his enemies, drives the Austrians before him, and defeats them again and again. Yet his ambition is not satisfied. More marvellous purposes crowd upon his brain. He will cross the Alps. He will carry the French eagles into the Austrian dominions. Proud Austria shall tremble for the security of even her hereditary possessions.

In these marvellous successes the odds against which he successfully contended will perhaps be better appreciated by referring to the following table, which gives the strength of the opposing forces, and the losses on both sides.

Parts of Campaign.	Forces.	Forces.
1st. Montenotte	French, 40,000.	Allies, 50,000.
2nd. Lodi	French, 40,000.	Austrians, 42,000.
3rd. Lonato and Castiglione	French, 45,000.	Austrians, 72,000.
4th. Bassano and San Georgio	French, 42,000.	Austrians, 56,000.
5th. Arcole	French, 40,000.	Austrians, 70,000.
6th. Rivoli	French, 44,000.	Austrians, 65,000.
7th. The Tagliamento	French, 70,000.	Austrians, 72,000.
Average strength to fall of Mantua	French, 42,000.	Allies, 60,000.

Average strength
during campaign   French, 46,000.   Allies, 61,000.

Loss during campaign French,   Allies,
          about 40,000.   about 120,000

These numbers include the French soldiers left in Italy to protect the French rear, and the re-enforcements that joined the Austrian armies after the battle of the Tagliamento. The losses include killed, wounded, and captured on both sides, but not the Austrian soldiers who died in the fortress of Mantua.

By a reference to the above table it will be seen that the average strength of the French forces prior to the capitulation of Mantua was forty-two thousand, while that of the opposing forces was sixty thousand,—a ratio of seven to ten. During this time more than one hundred thousand Austrians were killed, wounded, or captured by the Army of Italy, while the French lost less than thirty-five thousand.

Throughout the campaign, the average strength of the French forces was forty-six thousand and that of the opposing forces sixty-one thousand,—a ratio of about three to four. With these numbers Bonaparte defeated one Sardinian army and six Austrian armies; and killed, wounded, or captured, one hundred and twenty thousand men. During the entire struggle, each French soldier put *hors de combat*, on an average, two and a half Austrians; and forty-six thousand Frenchmen were more than a match for sixty-one thousand Austrians.

By skill in strategy and tactics Bonaparte was constantly successful in the face of these odds. By skill in strategy he outnumbered the enemy upon all the prominent battlefields except Arcole and Rivoli; and by skill in tactics he won these two battles.

At times the odds against him were almost too great to be overcome. In the Arcole part of the campaign the inequality between the opposing armies was greatest, and here he carne nearest to defeat; here, after desperate fighting, forty thousand Frenchmen, guided by his genius, defeated seventy thousand Austrians.

It was said by Napoleon that Masséna's presence on a battlefield was equivalent to a re-enforcement of twenty thousand men. Surely, when we consider Bonaparte's marvellous successes in the face of such great odds, we are led to reckon the value of his presence by still greater numbers.

It is difficult to conceive of any standard by which to measure the power of intellect. Mind cannot be measured with a foot rule. Only by comparison can we form a correct estimate of its power. By comparing the odds and the results in these operations, we can imagine Bonaparte's intellect exerting itself as a physical force, more powerful in the conflict than thousands of re-enforcements. In imagination we can see two opposing armies advancing to begin a great battle. We can see the brave soldiers of Austria, their glittering arms, and their old white-haired commander. We can see the French divisions and their eagles. We can see Massena, Lannes, Augereau, Joubert, and in their midst Napoleon.

The battle begins. The brave meet the brave. All are determined to conquer or die; all fight desperately, furiously. We can see the wavering lines, hear the roar of the cannon, the rattle of the musketry. We can see the troops hurrying hither and thither, and amidst confusion and death hear the shouts of victory. In the smoke of the battle we can now and then catch a glimpse of Napoleon galloping over the battlefield. He commands. He does not blanch in the face of great odds. He is master of the situation. His eagle eye takes in the whole field. He sees where the blow must be struck to decide the struggle. He gives the word. The reserves move forward; they charge; the crash comes. The Austrians waver and fall back; the French rush on with cheers. The smoke clears away; the conflict is ended; the battle is won.

Bravery did not decide this battle; for the Austrians and French were equally brave. Numbers did not decide it; for the Austrians outnumbered the French. It was the intellect of Bonaparte which turned the scale. Was not his intellect all-powerful at Rivoli, Austerlitz, and Friedland?

To conduct a campaign to a successful termination is a worthy task for a great intellect. It is difficult to conceive of any undertaking which requires greater and more diverse powers of mind. Hundreds of matters must be carefully considered. Not only the strategical and tactical manoeuvres by which he concentrates his forces and wins his victories, but his communications, his means of transportation, the supplies for his army, the equipment and discipline of his troops, the abilities of his subordinate commanders, the topography and resources of the country, give him the greatest anxiety. He must give careful attention to all these matters; for the neglect of a single one may lead to disaster. He must be brave, clear-headed, cool, cautious, and fearless; and be able to make a quick decision in critical times. He must have an eye for facts. He must weigh correctly all reports and rumours, and from the doubtful information at hand sift the true from the false. He must see everything that is going on around him. His glance must penetrate the enemy's line, his vision sweep the whole theatre of operations. Says Napoleon:—

> The first quality of a commander-in-chief is the possession of a cool head, which receives correct impressions of things, which never becomes over-excited, which does not permit itself to be intoxicated by good nor bewildered by bad news,—a mind in which the successive or simultaneous impressions received during the course of a day classify themselves, and take the only place they should properly occupy; for good sense and reason are the result of comparing several sensations, weighed with equal consideration.
>
> There are men who, by reason of their physical and moral constitutions, interpret every event in the same way; whatever may be their wisdom, spirit, courage, and other qualities, nature has not called them to the command of armies and the direction of great military operations.
>
> The commander-in-chief is the head; he is everything for the army. It was not the Roman army which conquered Gaul, but Caesar; it was not the Carthaginian army which, at the gates of Rome, made the Eternal City tremble, but Hannibal; it was not the Macedonian army which marched as far as the Indus, but Alexander; it was not the Prussian army which defended Prussia for seven years against the three most powerful states of Europe, but Frederick.

By studying the campaigns of great soldiers during different periods of the world's history, it is found that their successes are due, in great measure, to the correct application of certain unchangeable laws. These laws are the principles of strategy. They have been formulated after careful study of the manoeuvres and combinations of the great masters of war. Born of long and varied experience, and found immutable in all ages, they are the basis for all future successes.

Several of the most important of these principles are given here. The first three embrace almost the whole subject of strategy; and consequently include several of those which follow them.

First: Be stronger than the enemy on the battlefield.

Third: Operate upon interior lines.

Fourth: Engage your masses with the fractions of the enemy's forces.

Fifth: Divide the forces of the enemy, and beat them in detail.

Sixth: Operate offensively and in force along but one line at a time.

Seventh: Do not advance to attack with the main parts of an army separated by impassable obstacles.

Eighth: Concentrate an overwhelming mass upon the vital point of the enemy.

This last principle reaches into the domain of tactics, for it is applicable also on the battlefield. But on the battlefield tactics and strategy blend, so that it is not always possible to determine exactly the dividing line between them.

Owing to improved weapons of warfare, to better means of transportation, and to discoveries in electricity, changes in the method of applying these principles have resulted; but the principles themselves are immutable. They are the same today as in the days of Alexander, of Hannibal, of Caesar, and of Napoleon. They are the foundations of all great military successes. They are the test of generalship. No Commander can long violate them without bringing disaster and ruin upon his army.

Mankind is apt to measure a soldier's ability by his successes. As victory is the aim of all strategy and tactics, it is proper that generalship should be judged by the results attained. But this test is not always infallible. When a commander wins battle after battle and campaign after campaign under many difficulties, his successes are almost a sure proof of great generalship; not because they themselves are an infallible test of his military ability, but because they can be attained only by carrying out correctly the principles of war. But if we consider single manoeuvres, or single battles, the test of victory does not necessarily apply; for the commander may blunder into a victory; he may win a battle by tactical skill while his strategical manoeuvres have been a series of errors. He may even meet defeat without having committed a single fault in either tactics or strategy.

How then are we to determine whether a battle or a manoeuvre was conducted correctly or incorrectly? What is the infallible test of generalship.' The answer is. The immutable principles of war. He who follows them as far as possible in every step that he takes shows good generalship. To this it may be replied that the principles sometimes conflict, and that it is impossible to proceed without violating one of them; or that no general has ever conducted a campaign without sometimes violating some principle of strategy or tactics. This is true; a commander has often no alternative but to take up a faulty position, or to carry out a plan which violates some principle of war. Taking into account these facts, the following rule may be taken as the test of generalship: *To carry out the immutable principles of war when it is possible to do so; when they conflict, to carry out those which offer the greatest advantages.*

To operate always upon interior lines may be impossible; but if a commander carries out this principle when it is possible to do so, he is doing all in this respect that any soldier can do to win success.

In order to illustrate this subject by a particular case, let us refer to one of Bonaparte's manoeuvres in the Bassano and San Georgio part of the campaign. It will be remembered that he had two divisions at Rivoli, and one at Salo on the other side of Lake Garda. He had decided to take the offensive; he wished to advance upon Roveredo with these three divisions. In only two ways could this be accomplished: the division at Salo could either march around the north end of Lake Garda and unite at Roveredo with the divisions coming from Rivoli; or it could march around the south end of the lake, unite with the two divisions at Rivoli, and march on Roveredo.

Bonaparte adopted the first plan, and in doing so violated the principle of strategy that, in advancing to attack, the main parts of an army should not be separated by impassable obstacles. Had he adopted the second plan, he would have violated another principle. He would have exposed his communications to an attack in the vicinity of Brescia; and the Austrians could have descended on the west side of Lake Garda, and have attacked his communications without exposing their own. He had to choose which plan to adopt, which principle to violate. He chose the first, because of the two plans, both of which were faulty, the first offered the fewest disadvantages. Judged then by the test of generalship, the manoeuvre was correct. But the commander who violates a principle of war, whether by neglect or necessity, always gives to his opponent a certain advantage.

In other words the enemy may always profit by the mistakes of his adversary, whether they are unavoidable or due to poor generalship. Referring again to the case just mentioned, it has been pointed out in a former chapter how the Austrian general could have concentrated his army at the head of Lake Garda, and by this means have not only outnumbered Bonaparte upon the battlefield, but have defeated in detail the separated parts of his army. The unavoidable violation of a principle of strategy by Bonaparte gave to the Austrian commander great chances of success. The latter, however, did not have sufficient military ability to take advantage of the opportunity offered, but made the mistake of dividing his own forces, thus allowing Bonaparte not only to unite his divisions at Roveredo, but to defeat separately the two Austrian armies.

Let us illustrate this subject still further by taking other examples from this campaign.

On the morning of April 12, 1796, Bonaparte had La Harpe's and Masséna's divisions at Montenotte ready to begin the battle. These two divisions, numbering sixteen thousand soldiers, were opposed to the Austrian centre under Argenteau, numbering ten thousand soldiers. Beaulieu, the Austrian commander-in-chief, was between Genoa and Voltri with seventeen thousand Austrians. The remainder of the Army of Italy was watching and holding in check the twenty thousand Sardinians at Mondovi, Ceva, and Millesimo. This was the situation when Bonaparte fought the battle of Montenotte, and broke through the centre of the allies. Before the manoeuvres were executed leading up to this battle, he perceived that the Austrians and Sardinians were widely separated, and that the centre was the vulnerable spot in their long line. By political and strategical skill he enticed Beaulieu through the Bochetta pass towards Genoa and Voltri; then, before he could return to aid Argenteau, Bonaparte concentrated an overwhelming force at Montenotte, and crushed through the Austrian centre.

In these operations Bonaparte carried out the following principles of strategy.

First: He brought a stronger force upon the battlefield of Montenotte than the enemy. He had sixteen thousand soldiers, Argenteau but ten thousand;

Second: He attacked offensively and in force along only one line at a time. His remaining divisions were in front of the Sardinians acting defensively to prevent them from re-enforcing Argenteau. No French force was left in front of Beaulieu, because none was needed there. "The sole use of a containing force," says Hamley, "is to prevent a reunion of the enemy's parts. If it is not necessary to this purpose, it will be better employed at the point of attack." As has been shown in the first chapter, Beaulieu could not aid Argenteau by advancing from Genoa towards Montenotte; neither could he aid him in time by returning through the Bochetta pass, for such a movement would take several days. Before this time elapsed, not only Montenotte, but the battles of Millesimo and Dego, were fought and won.

Third: At Montenotte Bonaparte divided the forces of the enemy. Afterwards he beat them in detail at Millesimo, Dego, and Mondovi.

Fourth: Montenotte was the vital point in the long line of the allies. By concentrating an overwhelming mass against Argenteau, Bonaparte broke through the line, and thereafter from his central position had the advantage of interior lines in operating against the allies.

Every principle of strategy which Bonaparte carried out Beaulieu violated. The latter had under his command fifty thousand soldiers; yet he so scattered his troops that he brought upon the decisive point— the battlefield of Montenotte—but one fifth of his army. What made the matter still more humiliating was the fact that, under his immediate command and within hearing of the guns of Montenotte, were seventeen thousand brave Austrians, who were marching and countermarching in the vicinity of Genoa to no purpose, neither able to re-enforce Argenteau, nor able to hold in check any fraction of the Army of Italy.

If, in the Lodi part of the campaign, Bonaparte had not been delayed in crossing the Po at Placentia, he would have had great chances of success; for the Austrians, having to form front to a flank[1] in order to fight, would upon the least reverse have lost their communications. On the other hand, Bonaparte could have been driven back across the Po without endangering in the least his communications. His object was to place his army in such a position as to enable him to destroy the Austrian communications without endangering his own.

In the Arcole part of the campaign, Bonaparte attempted a manoeuvre very similar to this: he crossed the Adige at Verona, descended the river to Ronco, recrossed the Adige there, and attempted to throw his army upon the flank and rear of Alvinzi. In this position, as at Placentia, he threatened the communications of the Austrians without exposing his own to Alvinzi's attacks.

In gaining a favourable position for attacking the flank and rear of the enemy, Bonaparte had to make a flank march, and consequently had to expose his own flank to the enemy's attacks. But in each of these cases his flank was protected by an unfordable river; and because he marched rapidly, he was able to effect a crossing before his adversary discovered his plan. Nevertheless, these flank marches were attended with considerable danger. In fact all flank marches in the vicinity of an active enemy are dangerous; for a commander who gains a

---

1. See footnote 2, chapter 2.

position upon the enemy's flank must necessarily expose his own flank to the enemy's attacks. Even when his flank is protected by a river, as in the cases just mentioned, he cannot cross it in the face of the enemy without taking considerable risk. Had the Austrian army been assembled in force near Placentia, it could have defeated the divisions of the Army of Italy in detail as they crossed the Po.

That flank marches are always attended with more or less danger is probably the reason why Napoleon seldom made them in his campaigns. As a rule, he preferred to strike at the centre of the enemy rather than at his flank. By striking at the centre, he could separate the enemy's army into parts and then defeat them in detail. By striking at the flank, he gave the enemy an opportunity to concentrate. Even if he defeated one flank, he might drive it back upon the other, and thus have to meet both in a single engagement. Thus at Waterloo, had Napoleon attacked the right of the English, as Wellington undoubtedly expected him to do, he would probably have driven Wellington back upon Blucher, and would have had to fight them united. As it was, after defeating Blucher, he had to fight them united; but this was not due to any fault in Napoleon's plan. It was due to the inefficiency of Grouchy.

At Marengo and at Ulm Napoleon made a flank march, and struck at the rear of the Austrians, and at Jena he struck at the flank of the Prussians; but these cases were exceptional. There were excellent reasons for his adopting this plan in each case.

In the Marengo campaign, Bonaparte crossed the Alps over the Great St. Bernard pass, marched to Milan, and threw his army from the north upon the Austrian communications near Marengo. This was undoubtedly a hazardous movement; nevertheless, it offered, on the whole, more decisive results and greater chances of success than any other plan of operations. By adopting this plan he was enabled to receive a re-enforcement of fifteen thousand soldiers from the Army of the Rhine. They marched through the St. Gothard pass and joined him near Milan.

Nor was this flank march of Bonaparte, after all, so hazardous as it would at first seem to be; for though his communications by the St. Bernard were exposed to the enemy's attacks, he had a line of retreat to the north by way of the St. Gothard, which he could have utilized had he been beaten at Marengo.

In the Ulm campaign, Napoleon was opposed to the Austrians and Russians. The Austrian army was on the Danube in the vicinity of Ulm, with its front facing France. A Russian army, several marches distant, was on its way to join the Austrians at Ulm. In numbers Napoleon's army was greatly superior to the Austrian army. By a series of remarkable marches, the divisions of Napoleon's army proceeded from the English Channel, and from other points in the theatre of war, towards Ulm. Napoleon was anxious to destroy the Austrians before their Russian allies should arrive. Had he attacked the Austrian army in front, it might have been driven back upon the Russian army, and he would have found them united in his front. He therefore decided to march his army around the right of the Austrians.

By making this flank march, he succeeded in cutting the Austrians from their communications, and at the same time interposed his own army between them and the advancing Russians. In this case a flank march was necessary in order to divide the allies and beat them in detail. In this manoeuvre Napoleon was wonderfully successful. He captured almost the entire Austrian army before the Russian army could unite with it. The danger of these manoeuvres was lessened by the age and character of the Austrian commander, General Mack. Napoleon, however, took the greatest precautions.

In order to screen his divisions while they were making the flank march around the Austrian right, he directed a cavalry corps and part of an infantry corps to march directly towards Ulm. Mack, who had learned that large bodies of cavalry and infantry were in his front, was expecting an attack from that direction. He was greatly surprised when he learned that the greater part of the French army had slipped by his right and had cut off his communications with Vienna. The superiority in numbers of Napoleon's army over the Austrian army, and the great results obtained by throwing his army between the allies, certainly justified him in making this flank march.

It has already been said that these flank marches are always dangerous, and especially so in the presence of an active adversary. During the whole of Napoleon's career, none of his numerous adversaries ever succeeded in defeating him by such a movement. At Austerlitz the allies attempted just such a movement against him; and they were annihilated in the most remarkable tactical battle which has ever been fought.

In the Austerlitz campaign, Napoleon was opposed to the Russians and Austrians. He had marched directly north from Vienna to Austerlitz. His line of communications extended back through Vienna. His line of battle faced the east, and was parallel to, and but a short distance from, the road to Vienna. In order to face the allies he had been obliged to form front to a flank, and upon the least reverse would have lost his communications with Vienna.

The allies, who had just been strongly impressed by Napoleon's flank march around the Austrian right at Ulm, conceived the plan of making a similar march around Napoleon's right at Austerlitz. They expected to cut the communications of Napoleon as he had cut the communications of Mack. This being accomplished, they hoped to destroy or capture the French army. Since Napoleon had won such a great victory by a flank manoeuvre, why should not they also win by a similar manoeuvre. They purposed to do so. They believed that, by following in the footsteps of Napoleon, they could beat him at his own game.

Napoleon was quick to discover their intentions. From the movements of the allies, he saw that their object was to cut him off from his communications with Vienna. In fact, they undertook to carry out this plan within sight of the French army. Napoleon saw that they were making a fatal blunder by weakening their centre. He did not even strengthen his right to meet the attack of the enemy's left. He waited until the movements of the allies had progressed sufficiently, then he ordered his divisions forward. With his own centre strongly re-enforced, he threw his army forward, like a wedge, upon the centre of the allies, crushed through their weakened lines, and actually cut them in two. They were beaten on all sides. Great numbers were killed, captured, and wounded. It was a splendid victory for Napoleon. It was a terrible defeat for the allies.

During the battle, Napoleon showed but little anxiety about losing his communications with Vienna. The reason for this was that he had another line of communications with France through Bohemia. This line was perpendicular to the front of his army at Austerlitz, and was shorter than the line through Vienna. If the allies had succeeded in their plan, and had even beaten Napoleon at Austerlitz, he could have fallen back through Bohemia without losing his communications with France.

Why was the flank march of the allies so disastrous, while that of Napoleon at Ulm was so successful? The principal reason was that the allies attempted to do tactically what Napoleon had done strategically. The allies attempted this manoeuvre in the immediate vicinity of the battlefield. They were within sight of the French army. Their movements were seen by Napoleon. The intentions of the allies were almost as plain to him as if he had ordered their movements. At the very time that they should have kept their forces concentrated, they began to separate them by directing a large force to their left against Napoleon's communications.

At Ulm, when Napoleon marched his army strategically round the right of Mack, he was, during the critical part of the manoeuvre, fully a day's march from the right of the Austrian army; and his divisions were in supporting distance of each other. Had Mack marched against Napoleon at this time, the latter would at once have united his divisions for battle.

To conduct a strategical flank march successfully requires great skill, and to conduct a tactical flank march successfully requires still greater skill. Both are dangerous operations when conducted in the presence of an active enemy. By a flank march on the battlefield, or in its immediate vicinity, Frederick was often successful against an adversary whose principal aim was to take up a strong position and hold it; but against a Napoleon, all the skill of the great Prussian would have availed naught.

In the Jena campaign, Napoleon made a flank march against the left of the Prussian army, somewhat similar to that which he made against the left of the Austrians at Arcole. At the time, his army was superior to the enemy in numbers. A Russian army was on its way to re-enforce the Prussian army. He wished to annihilate the Prussians before they were re-enforced by their allies. Against the Russians and Austrians combined, he had just won the battle of Austerlitz. He was flushed with victory. He decided that he would take the risk of making a flank march in order to gain such great results. His wisdom in thus deciding was shown by his successes: in one month he annihilated the military power of Prussia.

Having digressed somewhat upon the subject of flank marches, let us return to the subject of strategical principles as illustrated by the operations of the Lonato and Castiglione part of the campaign. It will be remembered that Wurmser had divided his forces into two armies: one, twenty-five thousand strong, commanded by Quasdanovich, was marching on the west side of Lake Garda towards Mantua; the other, thirty-five thousand strong, commanded by Wurmser himself, was descending the Adige in two columns, one on each side of the river. In addition to these forces there were twelve thousand Austrians shut up in the fortress of Mantua.

To oppose these seventy-two thousand Austrians Bonaparte had only forty-five thousand soldiers. Masséna with fifteen thousand was at Verona and Rivoli; Augereau with eight thousand was at Legnago; Sauret with four thousand was at Salo; eight thousand were in reserve; and Serrurier with ten thousand was besieging Mantua.

To meet the advancing Austrians, Bonaparte made his first concentration at the foot of Lake Garda, in the vicinity of Lonato. Here he concentrated all his available men. Even the division which had been besieging Mantua was directed to this point. Why did Bonaparte select this point for concentration? And why did he raise the siege of Mantua? By pointing out some of the strategical principles carried out and violated in these operations, we shall be able to answer satisfactorily these questions. In advancing to attack with the main parts of the Austrian army separated by impassable obstacles, Wurmser was violating a principle of strategy; while his lieutenant, commanding his right wing, in advancing upon the French communications without exposing his own, was carrying out a principle of strategy.

At the outset, therefore, Bonaparte had two important problems to solve: he must, if possible, defeat the separated parts of the Austrian army before any of them unite; and must also prevent Quasdanovich from cutting the French communications in the vicinity of Brescia. As has been shown in Chapter 3, in only one way could Bonaparte solve the first problem. By making his first concentrated attack at Rivoli, he could have succeeded in defeating separately the three parts of the Austrian army. But to attack at Rivoli, instead of at Lonato, would have allowed Quasdanovich to cut the French communications in the vicinity of Brescia. Bonaparte therefore decided to make his first concentration at the foot of Lake Garda. By concentrating at this point, he believed that he could drive back Quasdanovich, make secure his communications, and prevent the twenty-five thousand Austrians on the west side of Lake Garda from uniting with the thirty-five thousand on the east side.

In the execution of this plan there was still another important problem which he had to solve. He could hardly expect to be successful unless he could bring superior numbers against Quasdanovich at Lonato. To do this, it would be necessary to raise the siege of Mantua, in order to unite Serrurier with Masséna and Augereau. To withdraw Serrurier's division from Mantua would allow the twelve thousand Austrians there to unite with the thirty-five thousand Austrians on the east side of Lake Garda, and together they would outnumber the entire French army: nevertheless, this was the best plan to adopt; for if Bonaparte were defeated while Serrurier was in front of Mantua, the Austrians would undoubtedly capture this division. To withdraw Serrurier, when the Austrians in Mantua were nearly starved out and almost ready to surrender, was a great sacrifice for victory; but in this way only could Bonaparte outnumber the enemy upon the battlefield; in this way only could he hope to make headway against such great odds.

The first principle of strategy is to be stronger than the enemy on the battlefield. This principle is the foundation of all military success. As the commander who wins a victory is necessarily stronger than the enemy, it might seem that this maxim means simply *to be victorious*. But it means more than this. It means that he should engage his masses with the fractions of the enemy; it means that he should make every effort to outnumber him upon the battlefield; and when this cannot be done, it means that he should take every possible chance to strengthen himself and weaken the enemy. That Bonaparte outnumbered the enemy upon all the important battlefields except Arcole and Rivoli shows how well he applied this maxim. But what shows it still better is the fact, that, when he fought his battles, he had every soldier there who could be spared from other important points in the theatre of operations. When he won the Battles of Arcole and Rivoli, he had brought there every available man in his army.

This is the test of strategical ability. He who fights and wins a battle with inferior numbers may show himself to be a great tactician; but if he has idle troops in the theatre of operations at the time, he shows poor generalship. Contrariwise, he who concentrates on the battlefield all his available forces, and outnumbers the enemy there, may show himself to be a great strategist; but if he is then beaten, he likewise shows poor generalship.

In the manoeuvres and combinations of Bonaparte throughout this campaign, the freedom from error strikes us with wonder. It is generally an easy matter for one with a fair knowledge of the science of war to discover and point out, after a campaign is ended, the mistakes that were made;

to show how such or such a plan would have been better than the one adopted; or how, by a different tactical formation, or a different strategical manoeuvre, different results might have been obtained. In this campaign there is no chance for such criticisms. Bonaparte made no avoidable errors. From a strategical as well as from a tactical point of view this campaign is almost perfect. It was by following the principles which he displayed here that he afterwards defeated coalition after coalition formed for his destruction; and it was by committing the errors which he avoided here that he brought upon him- self those disasters which caused his fall.

The only criticism which can be made—and that only in the minor details of the campaign—is that Bonaparte did not at the outset supply his army with pontoon equipage. Had he done so, he would not have been delayed in crossing the Po at Placentia, or the Adige at Ronco, and thus have been prevented in each case from capturing an Austrian army. It will be remembered, however, that in the earlier part of the campaign it was almost impossible for him to provide his army with pontoons. At the outset his soldiers had great difficulty to obtain even bread and shoes. Until these were supplied, other matters of less importance had to wait. Furthermore, the crossing of the Apennines was at this time engaging Bonaparte's thoughts; he did not realize that the Army of Italy would, in a few months, cross the Po, the Mincio, and the Adige. In this connection it is worthy of notice that in his subsequent campaigns he provided his army with pontoon equipage, by means of which he crossed some of the largest rivers of Europe.

On the Austrian side, all the commanders except the Archduke Charles not only committed many errors, but continued to repeat them again and again. The Austrians were always either too much extended, or separated by impassable obstacles. Throughout the campaign they advanced to attack the French with divided forces. This was their greatest error. It would seem that, after one or two crushing defeats, they ought to have discovered their error, and have abandoned this system of war. But the victories of Bonaparte taught them no lesson. They were wedded to the past. In the face of defeat and annihilation they clung to old military ideas. Even the campaigns of Frederick the Great had taught them no new military truths. Their whole system of war was faulty. They believed in scattering their forces. By occupying all the principal roads and prominent points within their theatre of operations, they expected to hold military possession of the country. Their system was to form a chain of posts,—a cordon,—extending along the line to be occupied, and by this means they expected to prevent the advance of the enemy.

Their plan of conducting active operations was based upon the same faulty method. They supposed that the enemy would, like them, scatter his army to hold his line; and would advance with it divided into centre and wings, or into several parts, widely separated, perhaps, by intervening obstacles. Their plan was to meet centre with centre, wing with wing, part with part. In their view, should the enemy be so foolish as to advance in force along only one line, their several armies would outflank him, cut off his retreat, surround him, and, by attacking him from different directions, force him to surrender. To surround the enemy was regarded by them as the height of military achievement; to allow themselves to be surrounded by him seemed to them the height of military folly. Such were their theories; such was their system of war. Though in this system there are some truths; yet on the whole it is one of the most faulty systems ever advocated by military men.

Diametrically opposite to this system of war is that of Bonaparte. Instead of scattering his forces he concentrated them. His plan was to mass them against some vital point of the enemy, and to attack him on one line, and in such a direction as to place him at a disadvantage. With one division, sometimes two, as a containing force, he held in check a part of the enemy's forces, and then concentrated superior numbers against his remaining forces at some decisive point. If the enemy's line was too much extended, he struck at the centre, and broke through it; then attacked and defeated in detail the separate parts. If the enemy advanced to attack with his army separated into parts by impassable obstacles, Bonaparte manoeuvred so as to crush in succession these isolated parts before they could unite. In this way, by fighting a part of the enemy's army at one time, he was nearly always stronger than the enemy on the battlefield. With him this was the important point. His rapid marches, his strategical manoeuvres, his combinations, were all made with this object in view. He believed that success in battle depended principally on numbers. "God," said he, "is on the side of the heaviest battalions." It is worthy of notice that throughout his career he never lost a battle in which he had a numerical superiority over the enemy.

Sometimes it was impossible for him to outnumber the enemy on the battlefield; then, by taking advantage of the topography of the country, as at Arcole, or by skilful manoeuvring, as at Rivoli, he was able to overcome the odds against him. In these battles he showed great tactical ability. It was there, with fate against him and disaster near at hand, that his military genius shone forth with its greatest lustre.

Bonaparte depended in great measure for his successes upon the rapidity of his concentrations. Had the Army of Italy been organized into one complete whole, instead of into divisions of about ten thousand soldiers, each, it would have been unwieldy and difficult to handle. But as the divisions were independent, and were commanded by able soldiers, they had great manoeuvring power. By his rapid marches Bonaparte made his concentrations; by his concentrations he won his battles. It was the marching as well as the fighting of his soldiers that won for him so many victories against such overwhelming odds.

The Austrians could not comprehend the manoeuvres and combinations of Bonaparte. They could not understand the reasons for his triumphs and their disasters. It seemed to them that he was violating every known principle of war, and in spite of this was everywhere victorious. He defeated their scattered forces in such rapid succession that he seemed to be everywhere. In the midst of the Austrian armies he would unexpectedly appear in force, crush the enemy with superior numbers, and in a few hours afterwards mass his divisions to strike him another blow at some unexpected point. To be surrounded by the enemy did not mean defeat to him.

At Rivoli he was surrounded on the battlefield by one army, and in the theatre of operations by three armies; nevertheless, he annihilated the enemy. In this part of the campaign, with only forty-four thousand soldiers, he killed, wounded, or captured forty-three thousand Austrians. His movements were so rapid, his blows so terrible and unexpected, that the Austrian commanders could neither fathom his designs, nor understand his combinations. To them he seemed to have no system of war, and no method in his undertakings. He seemed rather to be the incarnation of force, moving like lightning, and hurling thunderbolts of war against his enemies, till they were crushed, overwhelmed, annihilated.

In former chapters we have shown how Bonaparte, by following these principles, gained his victories; how at Montenotte he cut in two the allies, then held in check with small containing forces their isolated columns, while he concentrated an overwhelming mass, first against the Sardinians, and then against the Austrians; how at Lonato and Castiglione he took up a central position at the foot of Lake Garda, united his forces there and drove back Quasdanovich towards Salo, then concentrated superior numbers against Wurmser, crushed him, and pursued him towards Rivoli; how at Roveredo he united his three divisions, defeated Davidovich and threw him back into the mountains of the Tyrol, then fell upon Wurmser's rear, cut his army in two at Bassano, pursued him, and shut him up in Mantua; how at

Arcole, with fortune against him, he threw his army in desperation upon Alvinzi's flank, and after three days of terrible fighting against fearful odds won the hardest fought battle in this campaign; how at Rivoli in the midst of his enemies he, by tactical ability, turned disaster into victory, then without a pause hurried his tired troops towards La Favourita, where he won another battle, and then forced Mantua to capitulate; how on the Tagliamento he met and defeated his ablest adversary, forced him across the Alps, united the French divisions in the valley of the Drave, marched them towards the Austrian capital, and in the very heart of the Austrian dominions ended this remarkable campaign.

In these operations Bonaparte left nothing to chance. Fortune sometimes favoured him; it was sometimes against him; but calculation entered into all of his undertakings. He planned his manoeuvres and combinations with the greatest care. He studied the topography of the country. Upon a map of the theatre of operations he would stick pins of different colours to represent his own divisions, and the enemy's forces in their supposed positions. Then by moving these pins about he would represent the movements of the troops, and in this way would make his calculations and study out his combinations.

"Napoleon," says Jomini, "possessed in an eminent degree the art of concentrating, with admirable precision, upon the decisive point of the zone of operations, columns which had begun the march from the most divergent stations.

"Provided with a pair of compasses opened to a scale of seven or eight leagues[2] in a right line (which always implies nine or ten leagues on account of the sinuosities of the roads), leaning and sometimes lying upon the map, where the positions of his army corps and the presumed positions of the enemy were indicated by pins of different colours. Napoleon ordered his movements with an assurance of which we can scarcely form an idea. Passing the compasses quickly over his map, he judged at a glance the number of marches necessary for each corps to arrive upon a fixed day at the point where he desired to have it; then, sticking the pins in these new positions and co-ordinating the rapidity of the march that it was necessary to assign each column and the probable date of its departure, he dictated those instructions which would be, of themselves, a title to glory."

2. A league is about two and one half miles; so that the compasses, as opened, extended to about one day's march on the map.

Having once decided upon a plan of operations, every effort was made, every energy aroused, every nerve strung, to make the plan a success. Rivers were forded, mountains were crossed, forced marches were made, obstacles were brushed aside, everything was done that could be done to carry out his orders and accomplish his undertakings. He planned so carefully and calculated so accurately that he foresaw many of the obstacles which would be likely to arise in his pathway, and in advance provided means to surmount them. He had a wonderful foresight into future events. His mind seemed to comprehend the entire situation; seemed to grasp all the facts, and understand them in all their bearings; seemed to see just how certain results were to be reached, just what difficulties were to be expected and overcome.

At Austerlitz he issued a proclamation to his soldiers, not only promising them victory, but even explaining to them in advance the manoeuvre by which he was to obtain it. On March 15, 1797, the day before the battle of the Tagliamento, he wrote to Joubert as follows:

I calculate upon being in the defiles of Pontebba on the 30th.

At this time he had in his front the Archduke's undefeated army and the great chain of the Alps. He defeated the Archduke, surmounted the Alps, and on March 30th was at Pontebba with the Army of Italy.

The proclamations which Bonaparte addressed from time to time to his soldiers in this campaign are, for the purpose for which they were written, model productions. In these comments they deserve at least some notice. We give here the principal parts of two, the first of which was published to the army after the defeat of the Sardinians, the second after the battle of Lodi.

First:

Soldiers! in fifteen days you have gained six victories, taken twenty-one colours, fifty pieces of cannon, several fortresses, and conquered the richest part of Piedmont; you have captured fifteen thousand prisoners, and killed or wounded ten thousand men. Destitute of everything, you have supplied all; you have gained battles without cannon, crossed rivers without bridges, made forced marches without shoes, bivouacked without brandy, and often without bread. Republican phalanxes alone are capable of actions so extraordinary. The two armies which so lately attacked you with audacity are flying before you; the perverse men who laughed at your distress, and rejoiced at the idea of victory to your enemies, are confounded and trembling. But, soldiers! you have done nothing since more remains to be done. Neither Turin nor Milan is yours: your enemies still trample on the ashes of the conquerors of the Tarquins. There are said to be some among you who would prefer to return to the summits of the Apennines and of the Alps. No! I cannot believe it! The conquerors of Montenotte, Millesimo, Dego, and Mondovi are impatient to carry the glory of the French people to distant countries.

Second:

Soldiers! you have descended like a torrent from the summit of the Apennines; you have overthrown and dispersed everything that opposed your progress. Piedmont, delivered from Austrian tyranny, has returned to her natural sentiments of peace and friendship for France. Milan is yours, and the republican flag waves throughout all Lombardy. The Dukes of Parma and Modena owe their political existence to your generosity. The army which menaced you with so much pride no longer finds a barrier to protect itself against your arms. The Po, the Ticino, and the Adda have not checked your progress for a single day; these boasted bulwarks of Italy have been crossed as rapidly as the Apennines. Yes, soldiers! you have indeed done much; but much still remains to be done. Shall posterity say that we knew how to conquer, but not how to profit by victory? I already see you run to arms. Let us march. We have yet forced marches to make, enemies to subdue, laurels to gather, injuries to revenge. Those who have whetted the daggers of civil war in France, who have basely assassinated our ministers, who have burned our ships at Toulon,—let them tremble! The hour of vengeance has struck.

These proclamations refer principally to the recollections of former victories, and to the welfare and honour of France. They are forcible and eloquent. Though exaggerated in statement, their burning words filled the French soldiers with enthusiasm. In them may be discerned some of the fire of Napoleon's genius. "Napoleon has words in him," says Carlyle, "which are like Austerlitz battles."

Did Bonaparte follow in the footsteps of Alexander, of Hannibal, and of Caesar, or did he discover new principles of strategy unknown to these great masters? What was the secret of his successes? By a brief review of the methods of warfare prior to his time, we shall perhaps be able to answer satisfactorily these questions. By this means we shall certainly gain a more comprehensive view of the distinguishing peculiarities of his system of war.

In the days of Alexander, of Hannibal, and of Caesar, formations for battle were in large masses several ranks deep. The weapons of warfare were axes, pikes, javelins, swords, and shields. The tendency was then to take up strong positions, adapted to the numbers engaged, and fight there great battles, upon which often depended great results. The skill of the commander consisted in bringing a stronger force upon the battlefield, and in arranging his troops so as to present a formidable front to the enemy. From this time on the battle became a great tactical encounter between the opposing commanders. Each strove to detect a weak point in the adversary's line, and, by skill in tactical manoeuvres, to strike a fatal blow there that would shatter his formation. Having broken the line, the cavalry would pour through the gap and attack the enemy in flank and rear. In these battles, in which the soldiers fought hand to hand, the important point for the commander was to hold his ranks firm, and either be ready to receive and repulse the attacks of the enemy, or to advance with immense momentum against him. During these battles it was dangerous to withdraw or weaken any portion of the line; for a vigilant adversary could detect the weakened part, break through, and in detail destroy the forces of the enemy.

These great tactical encounters were always preceded by important strategical manoeuvres. The genius of the commander was displayed not only on the battlefield, but in the theatre of operations also. It was necessary that he should give the most careful attention to his communications, to the direction and rapidity of his marches, and to the concentration of his troops. His object was so to manoeuvre as to gain some advantage over his adversary. He might cut off the communications of the enemy, while he preserved his own; might surprise him by an attack at some unexpected point; or might force him to fight under such a disadvantage that defeat meant ruin to his army. Strategy played an important part in the campaigns of these great soldiers. The marching powers of Caesar's legions were as necessary to his successes as their fighting qualities. It was the strategical knowledge possessed by Hannibal, in addition to his tactical ability, which enabled him to maintain for fifteen years his position in Italy against the legions of Rome.

The principles of strategy have never undergone any change. The methods of applying them vary from time to time; but the results obtained from their correct application are the same at all times. Bonaparte made no discoveries in strategy; he simply applied successfully the principles already known. To divide the forces of the enemy and beat them in detail was correct strategy in his time; it was correct strategy when the great Carthaginian general crossed the Alps and struck terror into the heart of Rome.

The invention of firearms increased greatly the importance of strategical manoeuvres. Firearms increased the defensive strength of troops, and enabled the commander with small numbers to hold in check, for a time, large bodies of the enemy. He was thus enabled to mass his other forces upon some important point on the battlefield, or in the theatre of operations, where great results could be obtained by outnumbering and crushing the enemy. Thus the increased strength of the defensive allowed also greater latitude in carrying out offensive operations. As soon as positions could be held with smaller numbers, and lines of battle could be weakened with less risk of fatal results, manoeuvring became of greater consequence. Mobility became then an object in the organization of armies, and strategy increased in importance.

Neither Marlborough nor Frederick the Great appreciated fully the change that the invention of firearms was to bring about in the increased importance of strategical manoeuvres. Marlborough gave little attention to strategy. In fact the organization of his army was such that he could not manoeuvre or deploy readily. His army lacked mobility. He exercised his skill in selecting positions and in fortifying them. His genius displayed itself more particularly upon the battlefield. He was a great tactical captain. When the storm of battle was at its' height, and confusion and death surrounded him, he was cool, clear-headed, and vigilant. In the turmoil of battle, he would detect the vulnerable spot in the enemy's line, and, by massing troops there, would overwhelm and destroy him. "This," says Hamley, "was his special gift."

Frederick the Great was fortunate in falling heir to a thoroughly drilled and disciplined army. Having to make headway against superior numbers and several enemies at once, he saw that success must depend in great measure upon the superior manoeuvring power of his own troops. But he saw only half the truth. His attention was directed more particularly to outmanoeuvring the enemy on the battlefield. He gave little attention to strategical manoeuvres and combinations.

His strategy was often faulty. But on the battlefield, or in its immediate vicinity, he was a master. While the enemy was awaiting an attack in some strong position, he would march stealthily around him, and by striking him obliquely in some unexpected direction, or by attacking him upon an exposed flank, would roll up his line and shatter his formation. It was then that the superior fighting qualities of his disciplined troops carried everything before them and decided the battle in his favour.

"Moving round their slow inert masses," says Hamley, "like a panther round an ox, he found the unguarded part, and cast himself on it with all his force. The secret of his success lay not so much in judicious movements in the theatre of war as in the use he made of the flexibility of his army as compared with the armies of his adversaries. It was by his success in the fields of battle, rather than by his plans of campaign, which were often faulty, that he finally emerged victorious from the struggle, with a military renown unrivalled in his generation."

Frederick's army was organized into one complete whole; it was composed of an aggregate of battalions, each of which formed a fragment of the main army. Though it was an almost perfect machine, and had as an army great manoeuvring power, yet on account of the peculiarity in its organization it lacked that perfect mobility which has been found to be such a necessary attribute in the organization of modern armies. Had it been composed of divisions or corps, each capable of independent action, it would have had greater mobility, and would have been better adapted to the purpose of carrying out strategical manoeuvres and combinations,

It remained for Bonaparte to appreciate fully the increased importance of strategical manoeuvres due to the invention of firearms. In the province of strategy he saw a field for great improvement. The Army of Italy was well adapted for carrying out his plans. It was already organized into several independent divisions, each of which was commanded by an able soldier. As these divisions marched rapidly, they could, under the eye of a skilful commander, be quickly combined into a powerful army on the field of battle, or be as quickly dispersed to important points in the theatre of war. This method of organization gave to the Army of Italy great flexibility, without destroying in the least its cohesion in action. In Bonaparte's hands this army became a powerful weapon of destruction.

In former chapters we have described in detail the strategical manoeuvres and combinations by which he won his successes. It is unnecessary to repeat them here; but it should be remembered that only by the greatest skill in strategy could he overcome such odds against him, outnumber the enemy upon so many battlefields, and destroy in succession so many armies. He was a master of both strategy and tactics. Herein lay the secret of his success. It was his perfect mastery of the whole system of war which made his successes seem so novel to the soldiers of his day.

Neither the generalship of Marlborough, nor that of Frederick, approaches in this respect that of Bonaparte. It is only by going back to the campaigns of Alexander, of Hannibal, and of Caesar, that any parallel can be found with which to compare his successes. In strategical ability he seems to surpass even these great masters of war. Among all the campaigns of the great soldiers who have preceded or followed him, none will compare with this campaign in the brilliancy of the strategical combinations, or in the marvellousness of the results.

No just comparison between Napoleon and the great soldiers who preceded him can be made, without going far deeper into the subject than is our purpose in this brief account of his earlier achievements. On this point, however, the words of Professor Seeley, who cannot certainly be said to overestimate Napoleon in any respect, are well worthy of quotation here. He says:

> The series of Napoleon's successes is absolutely the most marvellous in history. No one can question that he leaves far behind him the Turennes, Marlboroughs, and Fredericks; but when we bring up for comparison an Alexander, a Hannibal, a Caesar, a Charles, we find in the single point of marvellousness Napoleon surpassing them all.

In this campaign Bonaparte began active operations on the 11th of April, 1796, and ended them on the 7th of April, 1797. In one year he crossed the Apennines and the Alps, defeated one Sardinian and six Austrian armies, won fifteen pitched battles, and killed, wounded, or captured one hundred and twenty thousand Austrians. He had never before commanded an army. He was only twenty-six years of age. Though he had received a military education at Brienne and Paris, had distinguished himself at the siege of Toulon, and had gained some notoriety in quelling a Paris mob "by a whiff of grape-shot," there was nothing in all this to indicate that he possessed great military ability, and would in one short year show himself to be the greatest master of the art of war.

As the knowledge of war which he displayed in this campaign was not due to his own experience, we are led to inquire how much of this knowledge was due to the experience of others, and how much was due to genius. In other words, how much was acquired, and how much was innate.

While in the War Office at Paris prior to taking command of the Army of Italy, Bonaparte submitted to the military authorities a plan for operating against the Austrians and Sardinians in Italy. He made a special study of that country from a military point of view. He studied also the political history, the kinds of government, the peculiarities of the people, their beliefs, their customs, and their laws. By means of maps and statistics, he informed himself accurately as to the topography and resources of the country. In fact he gave the most careful attention to everything which might have any bearing upon military operations in Italy. The campaigns of Hannibal in that country interested; him greatly; and as Bonaparte was a great admirer of this great soldier, he studied thoroughly these campaigns.

His life from the age of ten till he took command of the Army of Italy was devoted to the military profession. At the military schools of Brienne and Paris he acquired a military education. While at these schools he was fond of mathematics and history. Afterwards he became very fond of his profession. He took the greatest interest in everything pertaining to the duties of a soldier, and the greatest pains to master all knowledge pertaining to the art of war. For this purpose he read and studied the campaigns of the great commanders. The campaigns of Alexander, of Hannibal, of Caesar, and of Frederick the Great, as well as the campaigns of many other noted commanders, were familiar to him. He was a thorough military student. He read and re-read the histories of these great soldiers, studied their manoeuvres, their plans of battle, their victories, and their defeats. Everything that pertained to his profession interested him. No details were too trivial, no facts too insignificant, to be carefully weighed in his mind.

To military problems of all kinds he gave the most careful attention. In military matters he would assume certain facts to be true, then, reasoning from them, would study out the best way to arrive at certain desirable results. The lay of the land, the rivers, the mountains, the general topography of any portion of country, at once suggested to him military problems. Upon this ridge or that mountain side he imagined a line of battle; picked out in his own mind the strong places of the line; thought out how it could be most easily defended; how the rivers, mountains, and swamps could be turned to his or to his adversary's advantage; how re-enforcements from distant points could be marched to join the fighting forces; how much time it would take; how he could beat the adversary at such a point by such a manoeuvre; or how he would manoeuvre his own forces to counteract a concentration, or a charge, or a flank attack from his imaginary adversary.

"Napoleon," says Trevelyan, in his *Life and Letters of Macaulay*, "set himself problems at the opera while the overture was playing. 'I have ten thousand men at Strasburg; fifteen thousand at Magdeburg; twenty thousand at Wurtzburg. By what stages must they march so as to arrive at Ratisbon on three successive days?'"

"Unlike most army officers," says Ropes, in his work on the First Napoleon, "Bonaparte found in the profession of arms a profession worthy of his utmost devotion. He read and studied the great campaigns of the world. He wrote for his own use commentaries and criticisms on Caesar's operations in Gaul and Frederick's campaigns in Saxony and Silesia. Of every species of military knowledge he was a serious and accurate student. He was, moreover; as attentive to the dry details of the art as he was fond of studying the higher branches. No man in the army had a more sure eye for ground, could estimate more certainly what could and could not be effected by a battery placed here or placed there, whether a column of troops could or could not reach a given point by such or such a time. Nay, more than this, no captain of a company knew better than he whether the rations furnished to the men were what they should be or not. Napoleon to the end of his days was a good judge of the common soldier's soup and bread."

"Napoleon," says Colonel Dodge, "collated the knowledge of war which existed in his youth, and out of it wrought so perfect a system that he is the one captain whom all modern soldiers strive to copy."

"He was," says Lord, "a military prodigy equally great in tactics and strategy,—a master of all the improvements which had been made in the art of war, from Epaminondas to Frederick II."

It is difficult to say just what effect all this acquired knowledge had on the mind of Bonaparte; but it seems certain to us that his knowledge of the art of war was in great measure obtained from the experience of others. By studying the campaigns of the greatest captains, he laid the foundation of his own successes. Perhaps much of his knowledge was due to his solving those problems which his imagination suggested; perhaps much was due to his genius; but without the profound study and deep meditation of his youth, he would not, we think, have become one of the greatest masters of the art of war that the world has ever known.

The conditions for great strategical combinations are today superior to the conditions a hundred years ago. As firearms increased the importance of strategical manoeuvres in the past, so likewise repeating arms, railways, and telegraph lines have increased still more the importance of strategical manoeuvres in our day. The principles remain the same, but the facilities for applying them have greatly increased. In the dispatch of orders electricity has annihilated time; steam has revolutionized the movements of troops; and inventions have given to armies much greater fighting power. Better weapons of warfare always increase the fighting power of an army; they increase its defensive strength, and allow small bodies to hold in check for a time large bodies of the enemy. In this way they increase the manoeuvring power and offensive; strength of an army, and give to strategy a still greater value.

Another Napoleon will probably never arise; yet imagination can picture a soldier who, holding in his grasp the telegraph and railways, shall plan and execute as great strategical combinations in the campaigns of the future as Napoleon planned and executed a hundred years ago.

There are many lessons to be learned from this campaign; but perhaps the most important of all is that only by the deepest study can any man, however talented he may be, gain a knowledge of the science of war. He who would become a master in the military art must study deeply and think clearly. He must not only keep abreast of the military knowledge of his own day, but must study carefully the campaigns of the great commanders.

"I desire to say now," says General R. W. Johnson, "that the young officer who reads the most, thinks the most, and obeys orders most promptly, is the one who comes to the front when necessity calls for men. I mean men of iron mould and dauntless purpose, who grasp not after baubles, who bow not at the venal shrine of a false and prostituted public opinion,—men whose souls are not intoxicated by shallow draughts from the beaker of success, and who do not shrivel in the first heat of disappointment,—men whose spirits rise as adversities thicken, acquire fresh courage and sterner resolve with each succeeding failure,, confront new perils and difficulties, new foes and trials, with unquailing front,—men who gather to their hearts more of the light and essence of heaven as the world glowers and glooms around them.

"How many of the young men in the army or in civil life are destined to make their marks in this world, or to leave behind them the record of useful lives with no shame to remember, no wish to forget? Think of this, young man, and let your aim be high. There may be mountains in your pathway, but you will discover that with no more certainty do the recurrent waves wear away by ceaseless buffetings and gradual encroachments the granite of their rocky shores than do persistent effort and unswerving perseverance, when sustained by calmness, probity, and intelligence, wear away the rough places in life. There is no genius like the genius of labour. There is no reward like that which comes from energy, system, and perseverance."

When Bonaparte took command of the Army of Italy he seemed a mere boy. At first the soldiers had misgivings as to whether he could lead them successfully. But when the Army of Italy descended from the Apennines into the fertile valley of the Po, the soldiers began to understand Bonaparte. They began then to have faith in him. They could see in the features of the boy the genius of the soldier; and as victory followed victory their admiration for him increased. When he showed himself brave and fearless at the bridges of Lodi and Arcole, their admiration knew no bounds.

Ever after these events he was the idol of his soldiers. His presence filled them with enthusiasm. He retained throughout his career the extraordinary hold that he gained over them in this campaign. In triumph or in adversity, on the field of Austerlitz, or amid the snows of Russia, his soldiers never wavered in loyalty to him. Twenty-five years after this campaign as he lay upon his deathbed, his mind went back to the Army of Italy.

"Take this watch," said he to Count Bertrand at St. Helena, "it struck two in the morning when I ordered Joubert to attack' at Rivoli."

As death approached, his mind reverted to the days of his earlier triumphs, to the days of his glory, to the days when the lustre of his arms was undimmed and his star was in the ascendant.